DAKSHA M. PATEL

Order this book online at www.trafford.com
or email orders@trafford.com

Most Trafford titles are also available at major online book retailers.

Print information available on the last page.

ISBN: 978-1-4907-8950-7 (sc)
ISBN: 978-1-4907-8949-1 (hc)
ISBN: 978-1-4907-8954-5 (e)

Library of Congress Control Number: 2018948084

Trafford rev. 06/27/2018

Trafford PUBLISHING® www.trafford.com
North America & international
toll-free: 1 888 232 4444 (USA & Canada)
fax: 812 355 4082

To Rakesh's beloved guru, Brahm Swaroop Pramukh Swami Maharaj, along with Kekti, Bharat, Amrish, and other family members

Dance he did into hearts of each and every one he met

And in the end, it's not the years in your life that
counts, (but) it's the life in your years.

—Abraham Lincoln

Preface

This story is in memory of an extraordinary boy whose life was never about him, but about God and everyone else. The courage he showed during a difficult time in his life is truly inspirational, which needed to be shared, if for nothing else, for assisting others, young and old, who are in a similar situation.

My contact with him was very sporadic, to say the least, except for last few years. In order to write this memoir, I had to rely on others to contribute. Most of it is from people who had the personal experience and exposure to him. Others are from my own individual encounters, and most helpful was his almost daily tweets and some of the emails his mother, Ketki, sent me. As far as his friends and family, few contributed. Others were unable to do so, partly because it was too hard and painful for them to recite their memories of Rakesh.

Most of all, this book is about the extraordinary way he handled his three-year fight with acute lymphocytic leukemia, or ALL. That can serve many people who are going through similar issues. He was a great example of faith and trust, specifically how faith in God can help one through anything and everything in life. The book shows, future is not ours to see. All one can do is deal with what God and fate hands to him or her. Rakesh lived an exemplary life following that motto.

Acknowledgments

I am deeply moved and thankful for the friends and family members who shared with me the time they spent with Rakesh. This book would not have been possible without their help.

Chapter 1

The night of April 29, 1991, was ordinary, drizzly, and cloudy on Staten Island, a suburb of New York City. An ordinary baby boy was born in the middle of the night to ordinary parents, his mother, Ketki and his father, Bharat. No one knew it was not an ordinary day. It was a heavenly day. This baby was named Rakesh, and he had an older brother named Amrish.

Over the years, Rakesh was also known as Raku, Rocky, Rock, and Nanku, which means "little one." My favorite was Rock, for no particular reason. He was born into a family with deep religious faith. Just like all other parents and families, no one knew what his future would be, what to expect, or where his life would lead him.

Not knowing what to expect in New York City, Kekti and Bharat had kept Amrish with his maternal grandfather Pramod aka Papaji and Maternal Grandmother Nalini aka Naliba, my older brother and sister-in-law, in New Orleans since he was born there. He joined his parents in New York at the age of four, just before Rakesh was born.

To escape the New York rat race, Ketki and Bharat decided to move to Texas when Rakesh was six months old. There, they lived a stone's throw away from Ketki's uncle and aunt- Harshaddada and Sarojba, the second of my two brothers and his wife. The paternal grandfather Rasikdada and Grandmother Lalitaba, also lived with them. Extended family members living together suited Rakesh just fine.

Over the years, it became apparent that he loved all his immediate and extended family as well as whomever he came in contact with, more than any one I have ever known.

One day after Rakesh's death, I asked Ketki, "What was Rakesh like as a baby and during his early childhood?"

"He was a sweet-talker. One time, he did not do homework. When the teacher asked, Rakesh implied that the dog ate his homework. At home, he sweet-talked Rasikdada into telling the teacher when she called that it was true, that the dog ate it." But they never had a dog, so he did indeed have a mischievous streak as well. Then Ketki added, "He was a needy baby."

"What do you mean? Demanding?"

"No, he just wanted to be hugged at all times, and one could not pass by him without saying something to him."

"To me, it sounds like he was very affectionate child."

That he was. He especially loved children. He was a popular uncle among the children of his cousins. He was a man of few words, and it was hard to know his generous and affectionate nature. No one knew how deep the water ran.

His kindness was evident ever since he was just a toddler, when he threw Lalitaba's set of dentures in the toilet and flushed them. Everybody chalked that up as a rebellious act. When asked why he did it, he said, "They were hurting Lalitaba. Now they won't hurt her."

When Rakesh was a toddler and Amrish was in elementary school, we were all spending Thanksgiving in New Orleans with papaji and Naliba. After lunch on Black Friday, Rakesh said impatiently, "Let's go to buy toys."

I mentioned, "It's going to be very crowded today."

"No, I want to go now!" Rakesh insisted.

Finally I gave in and said, "All right," but I then added, "On one condition. I will buy you both any toys you want, but you have to pick out five toys each, twenty dollars or less to donate to Toys for Tots. And they cannot be battery operated."

Toys R Us was very crowded, as expected. I stayed close to them while they rolled the shopping cart around the store, but I didn't say anything. They knew I was nearby, but they did not look to me for help. Their conversation was like this:

"Hey, Rocky, make sure it's not battery operated."

"Look, Amu. This is a nice toy."

"Yes, but it's twenty-five dollars. Let's find another."

"How about this?"

"Yes, let's get it," said Amrish. "Rocky, we need to find something for girls also. Let's go to the girls' section."

And they very diligently and with great thoughtfulness did what I had told them to do. I was very proud of them. They did much better than

I ever did in previous years. I would just go down the aisle and throw in whatever seemed good.

At the checkout, I said, "Because of you two, ten children will have toys on Christmas morning."

They looked at each other, high-fived one another, and smiled from ear to ear. That became our routine for the next five years. His sympathetic and affectionate nature became more and more evident as he grew older.

To help out Ketki, I went to pick up Rakesh when he was in high school. He was waiting outside. Before I approached him, I saw him giving money to a girl standing next to him.

"What was that about?" I asked.

"She was hungry and did not have money to buy something from the vending machine."

I told that to Ketki. She replied, "He does that all the time to help out anybody who needs help."

He always spent more time figuring out how his toys worked or were made than he spent playing with them. He always appeared to be in deep thought.

Even though it was not obvious to the casual observer, he was close Lalitaba. When he was seventeen, his parents were visiting a sick friend one evening. He was alone at home with his grandparents. Raikdada, who was suffering from dementia, was sleeping in his bed. Rakesh and Lalitaba were in the living room. Rakesh was watching a basketball game, while Lalitaba was resting on the sofa and watching the game as well.

All of a sudden, he saw that his grandma was having a seizure and foaming at the mouth. His cell phone was in his room, so he used the landline to call 911. The operator stayed on the phone with him, so Rakesh could not go get his cell phone to call his parents.

When his parents drove up, an ambulance was in the driveway. Unfortunately his grandma died two days later from a massive brain hemorrhage. I thought that, as traumatic as it was for him to go through this incident, God had him at the right place at the right time. Normally he stayed in his room most of the time. Not being there for his grandma would have been devastating for him.

For the two days before Lalitaba died in the hospital, I did not see him talk to anyone. He just stood around and watched the activities. I was told subsequently that he was very poised and his speech was very elegant at the funeral. He was good at making speeches and emphasizing the good to be found in bad situations.

Amrish told me that, during the eulogy, Rakesh said that Lalitaba always watched Mavericks basketball games with him and she knew what was going on in the game. At his high school graduation, while taking a picture with Rasikdada and Lalitaba's photograph, I saw tears in his eyes.

Both brothers liked playing basketball. They played mostly street basketball at the temple grounds on Sundays or any time available, usually before prayer services. Rakesh also played basketball in high school. He was not a particularly great player.

Ketki told me, "He was a motivator and mentor for the team."

Rakesh carried his team to the state basketball playoffs in 2007.

About a year later, Rasikdada passed away. In his eulogy, he said, "Rasikdada used to tell me to ask Lalitaba to make *shiro*, an Indian dessert, because he knew Lalitaba would make that for Rakesh but not for him for health reasons."

Rakesh was Amrish's world. Amrish, unlike Rakesh is somewhat reserved in nature and not as social. But he loved taking care of Rakesh. When they were little, he would help Rakesh get ready for school by helping with shoelaces and making sure his lunch was packed. They watched out for each other. Both brothers campaigned for each other to whomever they needed, especially their father. Rakesh was also wise beyond his age, even as a young adolescent.

When Amrish was eighteen years old, he had a girlfriend his father did not approve of. Amrish and Bharat started arguing, and it became heated. In anger, Bharat said, "If you can't live by the rules in this house, you can leave the house now."

Amrish, very angry as well, said, "Okay, I will leave this house."

All this time, fourteen-year-old Rakesh was sitting there and watching them shout at each other. He finally decided to intervene. "Dad, you are angry. Go to your room, calm down, and go to sleep. Amrish, you do the same. You both are angry, and decisions made in anger are never good and correct."

He also had a deep bond with Harshaddada and Sarojba. Both are very religious, and their sons, my nephews, have joined the sainthood at the temple. So not surprisingly, my brother is very fond of Rakesh and Amrish. To him, they are grandchildren rather than grandnephews.

My nephew from my older brother—Ketki's brother and the uncle of Rakesh and Amrish—has also joined the sainthood. He knew of Amrish, who was born around the time he joined the sainthood. In this sector of Hinduism, once anyone joins the sainthood, he is not allowed to have any contact with family. They are in society and do religious and social work with all families except their own. To summarize, all my three nephews are saints, and the only grandchildren on my side of the family are Rakesh and Amrish.

Chapter 2

Rock and Me

When Rakesh, Amrish, and their parents moved to Texas, I had just moved from Louisiana to Fort Worth. It was about forty-five minutes from where they lived, so my contact with them was sporadic and brief. When I saw Rakesh for the first time, it was in my new home, which had just been completed. He was just a little baby, and I did not think anything special about him at that time.

He spoke very little around the house. He especially did not like to speak in the morning. He had a special bond with his mother, beyond the mother-child bond. They communicated with each other without speaking a word.

Whenever I saw him, I would say, "Hi, Rock."

And he would reply, "Uhm."

I asked, "What are you doing?"

But it was always the same reply, "Nothing."

But finally I realized that doing nothing goes along with basic Zen philosophy.

One day, he asked, "What kind of work do you do?"

"I am a doctor," I answered.

He had a surprised and confused expression on his face. "A woman cannot be a doctor. She can only be a nurse."

That kind of orthodox thinking must have come from his paternal family. He knew his paternal aunt, who was a nurse.

A few weeks later, he saw a white coat with my name and MD behind it. He surprisingly said, "Wow! You really are a doctor."

I had a suspicion that he was not convinced that a woman could be a doctor, let alone as smart as a male doctor until very late in his life. At a

6

later date, he found out that my practice was treating sick newborns. He thought it was just feeding the babies and such.

One day when he was in high school, while we were coming back from a beach trip, they spent one night at my apartment in Waco, where I practiced, before returning to Dallas in Amrish's car. While they were sleeping, I had to go to the hospital for an emergency. I came back before they left to make sure they were safe and sound.

I told him, "While you were sleeping, I saved one baby's life."

Once again with a confused expression, he asked, "How do you save a baby's life?"

He knew about CPR, but it didn't occur to him that babies also needed CPR sometime.

I used to come to Dallas to visit during his toddler years and would take them shopping. On one of those visits, Amrish, Rakesh, and I went shopping for toys. They knew they could not buy any toy that even remotely resembled guns, not even water gun. Both boys also knew that from temple teaching.

Rakesh was quick to choose the toy. Amrish was taking longer to select one. Raku went to the front of the store, so I went with him. I saw him playing with some display toy. So I went to help Amrish pick the toy in the back of the room.

Rock turned around and did not see me. He started crying and shouting my name. I rushed to get him, and while holding him, I promised him that I would never leave him alone. I think that episode was more traumatic to me than him. I thought, *How can I put him in that situation?* I can imagine how scared and abandoned he felt, even for just a moment.

One time, Amrish and Rakesh spent a weekend with me when Rakesh was around six years old. It was somewhat awkward since I never had spent time alone with children, socially and full time, as an adult. I did not know what to do with them, when to feed them, and how to entertain them.

We went to a PG-13 movie and then to the wax museum, where they made wax sculptures of their hands for their mother. We went to puttputt golf. They were excited about that, but I found out that they did not really want to play golf. Instead they just wanted to play video games. I am extremely opposed to video game activities, particularly involving destruction and fights. I made them at least play one round of golf, and after that, they could go to the video room. I made sure the game they chose did not involve violence or destruction. I think they had fun.

Later on, we rented a movie. Once again, I made sure it did not involve violence. Since I did not know what movies children like, they talked me into renting a Jackie Chan movie. I did not think it was about fighting until after we started watching it. They were smiling when I commented on it.

I had made pancakes, using buckwheat pancake mix, for breakfast the next day. They hated it. Rakesh commented on it years later when he was in college. It's true. Children don't forget anything. Also I made frozen mini bagel cheese pizza for lunch. Instead of cooking them in the oven, I heated them in the microwave. They became dry and hard to bite. It hurt Rakesh's baby teeth, and he could not eat it. All and all, the weekend went okay, but not great.

During spring breaks over the years, we went skiing a couple of times and took a beach trip once. During Rakesh's first ski trip, his parents, Amrish, and maternal grandparents were with us. He did not like skiing (actually snowboarding) much. He did not want to do it after a day and half. He hated the cold temperature. Though he liked sitting around at the dinner table and sharing old family stories, mostly about how I was a difficult child.

A few years later when he was in high school, he said to me, "I can go skiing one more time."

So we went skiing again. This time, his parents, Amrish, and two of their friends were with us. Once again, he liked family and friends sitting around in the evening, talking, or playing board games more than skiing.

The beach trip was with his one friend and Amrish. His parents were visiting India. Once again, he did not act like he was having fun. But just like Rakesh, the day we left, he said in the car, "I could have stayed a couple of more days." I would pick him up from school. I said, if needed any help with schoolwork, he was to let me know. He said he had a math project where he had to demonstrate proportion by enlarging any picture on a grid. He had picked Garfield and Odie. We did that project together, exactly matching colors with color pencils. He received a perfect score for the project, minus five points for tardiness. That was entirely my fault. I have been very clumsy all my life. I have that picture laminated and hanging in my bedroom in my Colorado home.

We did not communicate frequently. But he knew that he could count on me for anything and everything. Rakesh and I had a different kind of connection. I think we shared the same DNA, such as both of us are left handed and we have the same habits for concentrating and studying.

Rakesh's generous nature should not be mistaken as being a big spender. One day he was riding with me in my SUV. We stopped for gas.

When I was done, he said, "Dakshafoi!"

I did not want Amrish and Raku to call me grandaunt. I am Ketki's *foi*, that is, her father's sister. So both boys call me *foi* as well.

"That's too much for gas. You need to buy a Mini Cooper."

Raku was also technologically savvy. Even now when I am struggling with my phone or other devices, Ketki will laugh. "Rakesh is laughing at you from heaven."

No, I can just see him with an irritated look at me. "Dakshafoi, don't you know this simple thing?"

Chapter 3

Though he was born and grew up in the United States, his love for Asian Indian folk dance called "Rass" was evident from the day he learnt to walk. Since we are in the United States, only Indian cultural activity was at the Swaminarayan (a sector of Hinduism) temple. He took part in each and every cultural activity at the temple, even though it meant traveling to various states.

Whenever he visited India, it was for some festival and cultural activity. Of course, all involved dancing. He loved bright colors like lime green, red, pink, orange, and so on, the usual colors of the costumes they wore for dancing.

Other than folk dancing and deep religious faith, he loved Superman and Power Rangers, also similar colors of their costumes. As a matter of fact, he wore Superman pajamas until his last day.

He always said, "Don't worry about anything. Just dance."

After high school, he followed his brother's footsteps by enrolling at the University of Houston and lived with Papaji and Naliba during that time. His major was business communication and technology related to that. He had joined the Indian Student Association at the University of Houston as soon as he started there.

At home, he never talked about his school or activities, though he would tell his mother almost everything during phone calls. Through his mother, family members knew he had started an Asian Indian folk dance team at the University of Houston and competed in the state of Texas.

There, he met a fellow student, also of Asian Indian origin, whose major was biology and planned to go to medical school. Both climbed to officer's positions within that club. He was very active in fundraising and other required administration at that club. She also loved dancing, and she had competed in various dance events. But she did not know much about an Indian folk dance called "Rass." One of their mutual friends told her that Rocky was great at Rass.

She pushed Rakesh to create a dance team with her help. As co-captains, they created an Indian folk dance team, like the ones at University of Texas and Texas A&M. The team was named "Roarin' Rass" after the university's mascot, a cougar. She knew the nitty-gritty of developing a dance team and related issues, and Rakesh knew the choreography.

Social media was his asset. None of us knew what was he doing when he was in his room and being quiet. He was always texting. Yes, he was doing that. But it was not because there was nothing else to do. He was communicating with friends, helping them with their problems.

Within six months, their dance team advanced to competing all over the state of Texas. Once again, according to Rass members, Rakesh's greatest asset was his ability to motivate. He was the reason the dance team had advanced at the speed they did. He was not able to participate in an international exposition competition, which was in December 2011, which they won. The team gave the three-foot-high trophy to Rakesh in the hospital room.

In 2012, they entered for a national championship. Once again he played a role of motivator. Even though he could not participate, travelled to Michigan, where championship was and played role of supporter and motivator

Chapter 4

Late in November 2011, he had an auto accident. Someone hit him from behind. It was a fender bender, no big deal. Since then he complained to his friends about headaches and back pain. He went to see physicians specializing in pain management soon after the accident. It was suggested he get further studies, such as an MRI. Surely he was waiting to finish his finals before doing anything. But fate had different plans.

He was not feeling well in the last week of November. His friends later told us that, when they were visiting him, he would have bad headaches, to the point that he would kneel by the bed and bang his head on the mattress. He did not tell Papaji or Naliba anything about it. He was worried about finishing tests and the fall semester. Not to forget, he also had a national dance competition in the middle of December.

On December 4, 2011, he was sitting in the living room after dinner, watching some religious show on the TV by his grandparents. The show was prerecorded, same day or day before, and aired from India. Naliba noticed his hands were white as a sheet of paper. Then they started inquiring about his health.

Papaji said, "You need to visit a doctor."

Raku said, "After my test next week on Monday."

At that time, Papaji had to put his foot down and say, "No, we are going to a doctor in the morning."

His grandparents also found out that he was feeling so sick that he was having his friends drive him to school.

The next day, December 5, 2011, came. They went to a family physician, who also happened to be a family friend. After checking him, the doctor ordered some blood tests.

On December 7, 2011, Papaji received a call from their physician. He instructed them to take Rakesh to Methodist Hospital immediately for admission. Rakesh was at the school, taking a test. Grandpa called

12

him immediately and told him to come home as soon as possible. He was already on the way with a friend driving. He was admitted to Methodist Hospital in ICU for blood transfusions and further testing.

On December 7, 2011, it was a nice, sunny day in Plano. I had just come home two days ago after working the long weekend. I was trying to catch up with computer work. I was also trying to make homemade herbal hair oil for the first time. A big pot was on the stove at low heat, simmering over three to four hours with olive oil, water, and all kinds of different herbs.

At around 11:00 a.m., I received a phone call from Ketki. "Rakesh is in the hospital and receiving transfusions and more."

"When can we leave for Houston?" I asked.

"I am leaving the office in five minutes. I will go home, get my clothes, and come over to your house within one hour."

I turned off the stove and did not even bother to do anything else with the pot. It was December so I was not sure what kind of clothing I would need in Houston or how long I would be there. So I just threw in whatever I picked up from the closest in the suitcase and went out to fill the SUV with gas while I was waiting for my niece. We left between noon and 1:00 p.m. I was driving.

On the way, we talked about what could be going on. Was it accident related? Was he taking anything that could cause him to be anemic? She told me they had done a CT scan, and it was negative. She was in constant contact with her mom and getting updates. She also told me that he had an enlarged spleen.

Immediately my thought went back to the accident. Did he injure his spleen during the accident? And now he was bleeding into the spleen, causing him to be anemic and having low platelets. Even though I did not want it to be true, I kept thinking, *Could it be leukemia?*

Just at that time, Ketki told me they were also doing bone marrow aspiration and testing.

I asked, "Do you know why they are doing that for?"

She said "Yes, to rule out leukemia."

And then both of us sat in silence for a few minutes and made small conversation intermittently. Most of the conversations were speculation and hoping that all his problems were related to the accident he had. We reached the hospital at around 4:30 p.m.

When we entered his room, Rakesh was in bed, and his grandparents were sitting on the sofa. Four of his friends were there, two girls and two boys. Rakesh looked at us, obviously in pain, but his expressions did not change, and he did not say anything. I could see he was stunned, and for the first time, he could not figure out what was going on. He probably had an idea when they did the bone marrow biopsy. He had not eaten all day, and he was not interested in eating either.

One of his friends was trying to feed him with a spoon and saying, "He will eat for me." He finished half of what was there. We started discussing while Rakesh remained silent.

I asked, "Did you take anything, any medication or over-the-counter stuff?"

His friend said, "He was taking something called Safi, supposedly an Ayurvedic herb for acne."

Ever since he reached puberty, he had terrible acne problems. He had consulted different physicians for that and had been treated for it without any favorable results. His friends at the university had told him to try Safi.

I looked at the bottle. There was nothing in the ingredients listed close to Ayurvedic except for rose water. Then we all started thinking this might have affected his spleen, causing him to have all these problems. His friends immediately started researching it online. We found out, in addition to lots of junk, it also had arsenic, mercury, and other heavy metals.

Ha! Ha! There it is, I thought.

Heavy metals were known toxic substances for bone marrow and spleen. We discussed that. We all felt relieved, thinking that had caused his illness. I asked if his doctor knew about safi. He quietly said yes. Finally all of us left late in the evening, except for his mother, who was going to stay with him.

Knowing my niece and Rock, they probably talked a long time before going to sleep. My niece has shown an unusual level of strength since that day onward. I credit that to her deep, deeper than anyone I know, faith in God and Guru.

When I asked her about that night, she said, since we did not know the diagnosis, they talked about faith and engaged in prayers. Surprisingly all through these four to five hours we were at the hospital, not only did Rakesh have no inclination to talk, but so did Papaji. He had not spoken a word. All his life, he has been a quiet person. He spoke very little, and whenever he did, it is always meaningful.

At this time, I could sense that he was engaged in prayers and did not see a need to participate in speculations. Obviously he was very concerned as well. Since his son, my nephew, and Rakesh's uncle, had joined the sainthood, Amrish and Rakesh are the only two grandchildren our family has.

Chapter 5

The next day, December 8, 2011, has been etched on my brain like tattoo on skin. There was nothing unusual in the morning. After morning prayers and breakfast, around 8:30 a.m., three of us—Pramod, Nalini, and I—headed for the hospital, carrying breakfast and chai for my niece.

Nothing much had changed. Rakesh had an uneventful night, though his headache was just as severe and throbbing. He did not want to take any strong painkillers. Rakesh did not say much. When asked about the headache, he just shrugged his shoulders.

Once again, I remembered that it was morning. I should not expect any conversation. Around 10:00 a.m., I decided to run some errands and go to temple for a prayer session, which happens at 11:30 a.m. After that, around 11:45 a.m., I was at the gas station to get gas for my automobile before heading back to the hospital. I already had inserted the credit card and was just about to start when my cell phone rang.

"Where are you?" asked Naliba.

"At the gas station."

"Stop and come over fast. The doctor is here, and it's not good news."

I started the car and drove as fast as I could. I was not sure what the bad news could. Naliba had not said which doctor was there. Luckily I was able to navigate Houston lunch hour traffic relatively quickly and found parking easily. I ran in to the hospital and Rakesh's room in the ICU.

My niece introduced me to the doctor, the hematologist. Even though he had essentially explained the problem to the grandparents, Ketki, and Rakesh, he was kind enough to go over all of it with me.

He said, "Bone marrow has shown it to be acute lymphoblastic leukemia, or ALL, with blast cell count of 98 percent. Normal is 2 percent or less."

"What is the next step?"

"Even though I can treat this problem, I think we need to transfer him to the University of Texas, MD Anderson Cancer Center. They are much more set up to treat cancer. If he needs a bone marrow transplant, then he will need to go there anyway. I will let his primary care physician know so he can arrange for referral and transfer."

Although my brother and Rakesh had not said anything or asked any questions, I knew my brother was listening and trying to analyze all the information. Rakesh was hard to read. I am sure he was scared, but not knowing much about the disease, he probably did not have a handle on it. By this time, two of his friends were already in the room. They looked stunned and scared for Rakesh. They also did not know what to say to Rakesh or us.

After the doctor left, Ketki stepped out of the room to call Bharat, who was not able to come with us to Houston because of a work obligation he could not get out of. Besides, we all were thinking and hoping his problem was minor and he would be okay in a few days. Nalini and I joined Ketki after a few minutes in the hallway.

At that time, Ketki told me, "The doctor was nice enough to talk to me outside the room and asked if it were all right to include Rakesh in the discussion."

She saw no problem with that. She believed in being very frank and open with her children. Then she said, "I called Bharat, and he lost it."

"What do you mean? Was he angry?" I asked.

"No, he started crying." Tears welled up in her eyes.

In the meantime, Rakesh's friends went on Twitter, Facebook, and any other high-tech means they had access to so they could spread the news of Rakesh's diagnosis. Within two hours of diagnosis of Rakesh's ALL, the news spread to the temples, friends, and families all around the world, including India.

Immediately his friends told us they were getting lots of replies, asking questions and wishing well for Rakesh. The Guru in India was also informed of Rakesh's illness. Immediately arrangements were made for Guru to call Rakesh. In the meantime, we sat in Rakesh's room quietly, making small talk every now and then.

I was getting very anxious that we had not heard anything about the transfer or when they were going to do it. I was squirming, but not saying anything because I knew all of us were upset and I did not want to distress anyone further.

Besides, I knew, if I said anything, Nalini would get angry at me and tell me, "They know what they are doing. Do not cause any problems by making hospital personnel angry. It would make the situation worse." I can hear her words, though not spoken.

By 2011, I had practiced neonatal intensive care for close to forty years. And I have been on the receiving end of the sick neonates all those years via transfer from outside hospitals. I knew how the system worked. It was Thursday.

At around 4:00 p.m., I could not sit still. I was afraid, come an hour later, there might not be anyone at MD Anderson transport system to answer incoming calls. Even though it was a cancer facility, emergency transfers were almost nonexistent.

Without saying anything to the family, I went in the hallway. "When is the transport team coming?" I asked Rakesh's nurse, who was sitting just outside his room.

"Oh, we don't know. The request has been placed. They come when they have an open room. It could be two, three, or more days."

"Do they know how sick Rakesh is?"

To that question, she did not have an answer.

Then I told her very politely, not using my doctor persona, "Could you give me the transport office number so I can call them personally?" And then I added, "I am a physician."

She gave me the number, which I called from the hallway. My family did not know what I was doing. When I dialed the number, it was a referral service office and not the transport office.

"Hi. Good afternoon. I am Dr. Patel and aunt of one Rakesh Patel, who I thought would be transferred to MD Anderson this afternoon."

"Oh yes! I have a referral for him, and we were going to call Mr. Rakesh Patel on Monday and make him an outpatient clinic appointment. It may be for Tuesday or Wednesday."

"No! No! Rakesh—Mr. Patel—is in ICU at Methodist Hospital and receiving PRBC and platelet transfusions one after another. He needs to be transferred today."

"Oh, I did not know that. I will arrange for transfer as soon as possible. But I need further information such as address, insurance, and so on."

"Let me give the phone to his mother, and she will give you all that information." I hurried to the room.

Ketki heard the last part of it before I handed her the phone. When Ketki was finished, she said, "They will have a transport team around seven o'clock."

I was agitated but at the same time relieved that the situation was under control. I went outside to let the nurse know, this time not in so much a polite tone, that MD Anderson did not know of the transfer. All they had was the referral. And I had told them what the situation was, and they were coming this evening.

The charge nurse happened to hear the conversation and came rushing to me. She apologized and promised me that she would be on top of it until the transfer was done.

In the meantime, the lobby and hallway was full of well-wishers, friends, and relatives. So both Ketki and Nalini were busy talking to them. Some offered to bring dinner for us. Since most of them were female, my brother remained in the room, except when a few of male well- wishers came. He had to talk to them. It was chaotic, to say the least. Naliba had accepted the offer of dinner from one or two families to be brought to the house.

By this time, I was both emotionally and physically tired, and I started to feel feverish. I kept Naliba to leave for home since we would have to come back when the transport team came. She was angry at me, saying I was rude and would not let her greet and talk to visitors.

I thought, *Typical Indian culture. Why can't people understand that we as a family have just had a very traumatic day?*

But finally we left to go to the house a little after 6:00 p.m. Ketki stayed behind.

Chapter 6

W ithin fifteen minutes of entering the house, Ketki called and told us the transport team was on the way and would be there at 7:00 p.m. We did not stay to eat. We started back for the hospital.

After the ambulance left with Rakesh and Ketki riding with him to take them to MD Anderson, Papaji and Naliba followed them. I followed Rakesh's friends since I hardly knew Houston geography, let alone MD Anderson's.

It was a dimly lit, multilevel garage that smelled of fuel and oil in humid and hot air. The concrete floor was sticky. Only a few cars were there. We walked toward the elevators and walking bridge.

As we entered the building through the double doors, immediately we felt relief from the heat and mugginess. Not a soul was to be seen. It was very quiet and somewhat scary. All three of us did not know where to go. So we kept walking down the long, quiet hallway. All of a sudden, it opened up with elevators and a security guard sitting in the corner. She greeted us with a warm voice and asked if we needed help. Of course we did indeed. She told us how to get to ICU.

We took the elevators down the first floor, also known as fish floor. It was dimly lit. As soon as we stepped off the elevator, we saw a big fish tank, looking to me a saltwater aquarium. And there was another on the other side. Soft blue lights lit all the fish tanks. It was very quiet except for the rhythmic sound of the pumps in the fish tanks. The hustle of the daytime activities had died down. There were many chairs along the walls and also in the middle. They were all empty, but one can imagine them being filled with patients and visitors.

When we reached the ICU, Ketki was in the waiting room and told me the ambulance EMTs did not know how to get to the ICU, and it took time for them to reach the ICU. I figured they normally brought patients to the ER and not any floors.

We all met at the correct place. Rakesh did not know what to think or say. I do not remember him saying anything since that afternoon. At MD Anderson, after a brief visit, his friends hung out in the waiting area.

As I entered Rakesh's so-called room, it was more like a cubicle and one-third the size of the ICU room he was in at Methodist Hospital. The bed occupied most of the room on which Rakesh was lying, all of six-feet-plus body. There was a reclining chair for someone to sleep in and another small plastic chair. A computer was attached to the wall for nurses' record. Over Rakesh's head was the monitor hung on the wall. There was also a small sink free standing at the far wall, and at the side of the pillar, there was an open toilet, that is, no lid to cover it. The toilet reminded me of prison cells I had seen on TV shows.

The walls were bare inside the cubicle as well as outside. Inside it was very quiet. There was the occasional noise of a breathing machine breathing for someone in the next cubicle. Occasionally I could hear the telephone ringing at the nurses' station and a nurse answering it. We all left around 11:00 p.m., except for Ketki, who stayed with Rakesh.

That night was very important for Rakesh. At around midnight (around noon the next day in India, which was about twelve hours ahead), he received a call on his cell phone from our Guru. There was a technical problem. Due to sporadic reception for cell phones in the ICU, it was disconnected. But within a few minutes, the call came again.

Guru said just two sentences, "Rakesh, all will be all right. Do everything doctors tell you to do."

After receiving Guru's call and blessing, both Rakesh and Ketki felt a lot better.

The next morning at the house, Naliba called Ketki to get an update. Just at that time, I walked in the kitchen. Naliba hugged me, and both of us started crying.

"I was hoping that his problem was related to the Safi and he would be cured," she said.

"It has been known that *ALL* is 100 percent curable, and he will be okay. We just have to lean on our faith and Guru," I replied.

After consoling each other, we started to get ready to head to the hospital with chai and breakfast for Ketki and some favorite foods for Rakesh.

He had bone marrow testing that day, Friday, December 9, 2011. They also did a spinal tap, where they put a needle in the back at the lowest space at lumbar spine 3–5 and collect cerebrospinal fluid (CSF) to make sure the cancer had not seeded in the brain and spinal column.

After obtaining the CSF sample, they injected medicine, a chemotherapy drug named methotrexate, to treat any possible cancer that had made its way into the brain and spinal column. Hmm! I seemed to remember studying methotrexate over fifty years ago.

Is this progress? I thought. *I think not.*

The physician assistants, or PAs, usually manage the protocols and did the procedures, of course under the umbrella of the attending physician. This was the first of many spinal chemotherapy treatments he would have. They were not going to start any other chemotherapy until after the second bone marrow results.

By midafternoon on Friday, Bharat and Harshaddada and Sarojba arrived from Dallas. Rakesh's headache was just as bad. But he did not want any strong medication.

When time came to leave, I asked Ketki, "Why don't you go home? I will spend the night with Rakesh."

Ketki looked at me with weary eyes shadowed by deep circles. She nodded yes, as if she didn't have the strength to even utter the word.

The night was uneventful. When we were alone, he told me to tell him some good stories. I don't even remember what story of my past I told him. He always liked to hear about past family stories. I fell asleep a little after he drifted off.

In the morning, some activity woke me up. "What's going on?" I asked. It was 5:00 a.m.

"Nothing. I am drawing some blood for the test," the phlebotomist, one who draws blood, said.

"Okay."

Thirty minutes later, the nurse came in to start his blood transfusion. She told me, "His hemoglobin and platelets are low."

I thought sarcastically, *Is that new news?*

Then I started gently rubbing Rakesh's forehead and head to sooth his headache. He seemed to like it. He kept his eyes closed. I guess, even though there was no bright light in the room, it helped him relax better. I kept rubbing his head, standing by his right side.

Two hours passed by. It was close to 8:00 a.m.

Rakesh opened his eyes and asked, "When is Mom coming?"

"I don't know."

I called home from my cell phone. Bharat answered.

I asked him, "What is Ketki doing?"

He said, "She's getting ready to come over."

"Tell her Rakesh is asking for her."

After Ketki came, I left for home. Rakesh was to move to the leukemia floor that day.

After I left, he told Ketki, "Mom, Dakshafoi stood here for three hours and rubbed my head."

That morning, by the time the family made its way to hospital, he was already on the leukemia floor. That evening, one of the research coordinators came to speak to Rakesh and family. He talked about research protocols. Ketki, Bharat, and Rakesh agreed to be part of a research protocol. I did not have any objection either since it was just a different schedule and dosing protocols.

One of the family friends from our temple was working at the MD Anderson bone marrow testing laboratory. She told Ketki, "Usually on the weekends, process is slow, but I will personally make sure that you have results by Sunday."

Many visitors started pouring in from Dallas as well as the Houston areas. It was very congested inside Rakesh's room and outside in the hallway and waiting area. It was very hard to control the number of visitors in the room.

He also had very important visitors on Saturday, December 10, 2011. The saints from the temple with God's Murti (known as "Thakorji") came to visit and give him blessings. From his tweet I read, I think that visit was very important and calming to him.

Taking chai and breakfast became routine for me while Rakesh was in the hospital. Papaji and Naliba came by with lunch around noon. We all normally stayed until after dinner. That routine continued until the end.

On Sunday morning, December 11, 2011, the attending doctor and his staff made rounds. Nothing was unusual. They discussed the process and answered the questions anyone had. One of the things noticeable about the attending doctor was that he had many pins on his white coat. I couldn't help but ask about methotrexate, an age-old medicine, still being used as a main approach to protocol. He agreed with me that methotrexate still was considered effective chemotherapy.

In the afternoon, in the midst of tension and worry, a very funny episode happened. Rakesh's headache was so bad that he agreed to take morphine for the first time.

Oh boy! Nobody expected the reaction he had. After morphine was given, he started laughing, giggling, and talking silly. He asked where his boys, meaning his friends, were. They were hanging around in the waiting room.

I went and told them, "Rakesh is asking for you."

When they came to the room, they could not believe their eyes and ears. Ketki made sure she took video on her iPad to share with all of the family. This lasted about thirty minutes. We all had fun laughing at him and laughing with him. I don't remember for sure, but I don't think he took morphine or any other narcotics until the last few days of his life.

On the next day, December, 12, 2011, he was to start his chemotherapy as soon as the bone marrow test confirmed the diagnosis of ALL. The attending doctor was making rounds. After discussing and answering questions, the attending doctor was about to leave, when Bharat asked, "If you don't mind answering this question, I am curious about the pins you have on your coat."

The doctor started telling about each of the pins and the last one. "This one is from Tulane University."

"Wait a minute!" Ketki interrupted him. "Are you from New Orleans? And your father-in-law is so-and-so?"

"Yes."

"I am Ketki. My father and mother are very good friends of your in-laws. I believe my parents attended your wedding reception, and your in-laws attended our wedding reception in New Orleans."

He remembered them. He called my brother "Uncle." Ketki and I made sure he would be Rakesh's primary oncologist (cancer specialist). I considered that as a miracle because even though he took care of Rakesh as an outpatient, the multiple times Rakesh had been admitted to the hospital, he was never his attending again. I believe it was God making sure that Rakesh got taken care of by someone we all would have faith in and were comfortable with.

Chapter 7

❦

His first chemo started very late in the day on December 14. Initially he received chemo almost every other day, both intravenous and a couple of times a week via spinal tap. He had a central venous line placed through the vein on his right upper arm, and family members were trained in taking care of the central line and changing dressings. He was to receive his chemo via central line.

On December 20, 2011, he was discharged from MDA and received his chemo as an outpatient. He stopped, took a deep breath, opened his arms, and said, "Outside world. Outdoors!"

He normally preferred indoors over outdoors, except for specific activities. I thought, *How we go on living life, taking so many things for granted, until that is taken away.*

The very next day, he had to go for outpatient testing, chemo, and transfusions, if needed. He had a very long day. In addition to being tired, he vomited on the way home, his first since chemo was started. Amazingly he had very few of those during his long, protracted chemotherapy. His main issue was a very sore, raw throat, which was painful as well as limiting his food intake. By reading his tweets, I found out that he ate whenever he could. Naliba and friends made his favorite foods for him.

Amazingly, he kept his poise and did not complain about anything, even at the hospital. Sometime I would get upset with the nurses for something or other. At that time, looking at me, Rakesh would raise his index finger, put it over his mouth, and then point his finger toward the chair in the corner. And he'd open his big eyes even wider. He was a popular patient. Even during clinic visits or a delay in test results, procedures, or chemo, he would not show any restlessness or say anything about it.

When at home, he kept to himself in the room. Visits from his friends were few and far apart since the number of visitors was restricted. I was worried about him being depressed. Though now we all know that he was

24

never alone. With social media, his friends were in constant touch. He had a favorite cousin, and he loved her two daughters. He did FaceTime with them a lot.

Two days later, Ketki and I went back to Plano. I had to go to work for Christmas. And as I entered my Plano home, I noticed that the pot I had left as-is had mildew in the oil, pot, and spoon. I proceeded to throw out everything, including the pot and spoon.

During his ongoing chemo, he was readmitted several times for testing and antibiotics treatment, any time he had a hint of fever. The family was trained to administer intravenous antibiotics, which allowed him to be discharged as soon as his fever subsided.

His father and brother were in Houston, while Ketki made quick trip to Dallas with me. Ketki and I came back on December 31, and I left the next day to work the weekend.

This time, Amrish needed attention. He had oral/dental surgery, hopefully the last of many procedures, for he had injured his teeth while playing baseball with his maternal uncle while in junior high. In the meantime, Rakesh was back in the hospital for fever and significant weakness. He also was feeling down.

Amrish had surgery on January 6, 2012, and all went well with no problems. But Rakesh had complications of irregular heart rate and restless night, and his sore throat was so bad that it hurt just to have ice chips in his mouth.

By now, he had two more bone marrow tests. It was showing progressively downward trending blast cells. The last one had 5 percent blast cells.

January 11 was another bone marrow test. Blast cells were 2 percent, quite a change from 98 percent on December 8. Exactly thirty-four days after the diagnosis of ALL, he was declared in remission. Of course, he had still to undergo a long, protracted course of chemotherapy. His day-to-day management was left up to Papaji and Naliba.

He had many ER visits and admissions, in addition to his visits to the clinic for testing, transfusions, and chemo. Whenever he was admitted to the hospital, Ketki and I would go down to Houston, and I would manage going to work from there while Ketki spent all of her time round the clock in hospital until he was discharged. And then she either would go back with me or by bus, if I were working. She and Bharat took turns for hospital times to accommodate their work schedule and needs.

Rakesh was very strong and tolerated all his problems—headaches, nausea, weakness, tingling, and numbness—all side effects of chemotherapy.

He never complained. He took positives, like when he was able to eat and the various foods he ate. All his tweets were cheerful, no matter what. Like after noting what was wrong, he would say, "ALL is well."

This is the acronym for acute lymphoblastic leukemia. He used it also for "all" as everything. He also tried to help around the house as needed when he felt well enough and had strength. Though getting admitted repeatedly for fever and headaches was wearing on him. I could tell from reading his emails. Also it was evident that he had not lost his faith in Guru and God.

He was admitted at least nine times during 2012, not including long, grueling days at the clinic for blood testing, spinal taps, and/ or transfusions. It seems that his headaches never subsided. He never took anything stronger than a Tylenol, except occasionally when he had morphine. The times he took morphine can be counted with fingers on one hand and still have a couple of digits left. He had repeated CT scans to diagnose the cause for headaches, but they did not find any obvious cause.

On August 1, 2012, he was admitted to the hospital, once again for fever. Ketki and I reached Houston by that afternoon. I had a rule that he was not to be left alone, no matter what, the promise I gave him in a toy store during his toddler years.

On August 2, 2012, I received a call from my partner's daughter at around midnight. "Dr. Patel, you must come over to cover the unit. My daddy is sick and in pain."

My first thought was, *Oh my God! He had a heart attack!*

I started to ask her about what was wrong. But all she said was, "He is hurting."

By that time, my partner came on the phone. "It's my gallbladder, and I need surgery for that." Then he added, "I cannot take any narcotics until you get here, and the regular pain medicine is not working."

Since it was midnight, I thought it would not be a good idea for me to drive. I said, "I will leave early morning and get there by midmorning."

He replied, "That's fine."

I somewhat felt bad for him and wished he would have called earlier. The next morning after I went, I saw him in the unit, waiting on me.

I asked, "What are you doing in here?"

He said, "My surgeon would be upset if he knew that I was not confined to my room."

He had surgery before noon on August 3. He was discharged from the hospital later that evening to recover at home. That evening, I called Ketki to tell her what my partner had done.

But she stopped me and said, "Rakesh is in the ICU, and he is paralyzed. He is doing okay, but they want to keep close watch in case the paralysis would make him stop breathing."

I was in a bind. My partner was recovering from surgery and still on pain medications.

Ketki told me, "I will keep you updated if it gets any worse."

The next morning, I got up 5:00 a.m., as that was my routine anyway. After one look at me, the nurses knew something was wrong. I told them about Rakesh. My body was there, but my heart was at MD Anderson. I proceeded to check babies and do my work. Luckily we were not too busy.

With the help of a neonatal nurse practitioner, I finished my work by 10:00 a.m. About an hour later, I called my partner and told him the situation. And I told him that all babies were fine and there was nothing to do but be available for emergencies. He came over within thirty minutes. He was hurting, but not quite as intense. He could manage. I left for Houston, feeling guilty that I had to leave my partner when he was not 100 percent.

Three hours later, I entered Rakesh's ICU cubicle. I saw Rakesh sitting up in the bed, and he was able to move. It was getting better by the minute. For the first time in the last eighteen hours, I breathed.

I told Rakesh, "It looks like you had a TIE (a transient ischemic episode)."

Rakesh, as usual, looked at me with an expression that said, "Whatever."

In a few minutes, his primary oncologist came by for a friendly visit. "I have reviewed your chart, and its looks like you had TIE."

Rakesh smiled and pointed at me. "She is smart."

Oh by George! I thought. *Finally he's convinced that I am a real doctor.*

He underwent many tests to find out the cause for paralysis, including a MRI. The next day, he was moved back to a regular floor. That day, Ketki received a text massage from the PA, stating that the MRI showed that paralysis was related to the methotrexate.

Ketki called home and told us about the results. We all took a deep breath. It was decided that he would not get methotrexate during spinal taps, and as a result, the frequency of the spinal tap would be decreased as well.

The next day, he was moved out of ICU. A day later, I went to breakfast with Ketki around 9:00 a.m. The attending physician for that month was doing rounds. Apparently she had not reviewed his chart and did not know the MRI results. She started talking about a psychology consult.

"But the MRI was abnormal and related to methotrexate," Ketki interrupted the attending doctor.

The doctor somewhat stopped and looked confused. "I was not aware of that."

I was very upset at her.

After she left, Rakesh asked us, "Do they think I am koo-koo?"

I could not stand looking at his sad face. After that, he went in the shower and stayed for a long time. I was very angry at the physician's poor bedside manners. It turned out that Bharat was not happy with that doctor either. He went as far as making a complaint against her, and it was decided that she would not be an attending physician for Rakesh again.

During 2012, Rakesh visited his parents and friends in Dallas whenever he felt well enough. His attending oncologist had arranged for the oncologist he knew in Dallas to monitor Rakesh and do the blood testing. They had mutual understanding that, since he was in a research protocol, in case any treatment was needed, including blood product transfusions, Rakesh must return to Houston immediately for that, which included hospital admission, if needed. It seemed he was in Dallas in 2012 at least twice.

One of those days, he told me, "I would like to go skiing one more time."

"We will go when you are all better. By that time, my home in Colorado will be finished."

In the meantime, Amrish was well into his study to become a pharmacist, his lifelong goal and for which he worked very hard. From Rakesh's almost daily tweets, I could tell he was happiest when his brother was visiting. Amrish made as many visits he could between his pharmacy school and little brother.

During conversations with Ketki, she told me that Rakesh was heavily involved in doing all the research about his disease that he could. I had given him a book about cancer, where it talked about "renegade cells."

One day, I heard him talking to someone on the phone and trying to explain cancer to that person and explaining like it was in that book. "Cancer happens when one of your cells in the body becomes renegade and multiplies as abnormal cells, affecting your blood or body organs. It becomes a tumor."

In hindsight, my fear of him being depressed was not necessarily true. Quietly, he kept doing what needed to be done, including studying his own illness.

On August 17, 2012, he had a bone marrow test. And minimal residual disease (MRD) was negative, the first time since diagnosis. That's when I knew we were on the correct path. He had continued to go to temple whenever he was home and feeling well. From the temple, saints came and visited him at home on September 23, 2012.

He was very pleased with the interactions with them. His intensive chemo continued, though it had to be delayed a couple of times initially for extremely low blood count. He also had been receiving transfusions as an outpatient or in the hospital.

On December 21, 2012, he was done with intensive chemotherapy, exactly one year and one week after the first chemotherapy. He was officially "in remission". Though he had periodic clinic visits for testing and occasionally for transfusion, if needed. He was also doing low-dose oral chemo at home. His liver was severely damaged, and because of that, he had to skip or delay taking chemo, as the doctor or PA directed.

Chapter 8

On January 2013, he was cleared to return to school. He jumped in with both feet to finish his bachelor's degree. He finished eighteen months' worth of study in twelve months. In December 2013, he received a BBA in management information system.

He was concentrating on working hard during 2013 that he had only one tweet in August, stating all blood work looked good and there was no relapse of ALL. In August 2013, Ketki, Bharat, Papaji and Naliba went to India for about ten days or so. I stayed with him, except for going to work. At that time, Harshaddada and Sarojba from Dallas came to stay with him. He was alone for one night and one morning until I returned from work. Even though he was doing well and did not need my help, I was not going to leave him alone, as I had promised in the toy store when he was a toddler.

In October 2013, there was an engagement party for Amrish and his wife-to-be, Krishma, in Dallas. Rakesh and the rest of the family members were there at that time. He looked so happy and elated for his brother.

By this time, he had already decided to become a PA and help other cancer patients. He thought, since he had gone through the same things other patients were enduring, he could help them in many different ways. In early 2014, he enrolled in a local community college to finish his prerequisite courses for PA school. He also took a job as a medical script writer at a local hospital emergency room, where he transcribed physician notes. He had very odd schedules, and sometimes he had to work all night as well.

He continued to be supportive and a mentor for his dance team. Even though he could not dance at competition level, he constantly saw the team during practices and meetings whenever he could physically, providing constant motivation. He even made trips to Michigan with the dance team and Arizona to visit his friends, cousin, and nieces.

Chapter 9

H e was already preparing for the PA school and had already drafted an essay, a personal statement, which was required as a part of the application, stating his reason for becoming a PA and his ultimate goals. Here it is.

There I lay, unable to move a single limb from my neck down, wondering if I would ever live to see the next day. My eyes were closed, thinking about what would happen to me next. I was terrified to say the least, feeling like all four walls in my ICU room were slowly closing in on me. I was able to comprehend everything around me, but was not able to respond in any way. Finally, I opened my eyes, and there she stood, Alexis Geppner, a physician's assistant (PA) who had been on my service. She came inside, put her hand on my head, and said, "Everything is going to be okay. You will be just fine." For some reason, I felt the utmost peace throughout my body and knew that I would be better in no time. It was then that I realized that I too want to make a patient feel the same way that I felt at that moment. I too wanted to make a difference in someone's life. I wanted to be a physician's assistant.

On December 8, 2011, I was diagnosed with acute lymphoblastic leukemia. That day marked the start of a one-and-half-year journey for me, a journey that was accompanied by family, friends, and, most importantly, a team of physician's assistants. It was these PAs that guided me through my treatment, and without them, there is a good chance that I wouldn't be writing this personal statement. There were times where the chemotherapy that I went through was just too much to handle and I wanted to give up, letting it take over me. The PAs at MD Anderson connected with me on a personal level. They pushed me to fight back and never give up. It is because of them that I was able to truck through my treatment and am currently in remission.

I can vouch for all patients when I say that, aside from medical care, a patient wants to see that his or her medical professional legitimately cares for him or her. From a patient's perspective, patient care is by far the most important aspect a medical professional possesses. You may be the most knowledgeable doctor in the world, but if you do not have a strong connection with your patient, your work is considered zero in his or her mind.

Through my one and a half years of treatment, I encountered many medical professionals, some of who cared for their patients and others who frankly didn't. It's the ones that care for their patients that are remembered forever. In becoming a PA, I want to make that impact on someone's life. I want to be able to make a difference in a patient's life, solely because I know it is every patient's desire to have someone care for him or her in a time of need. I want to be able to leave that lasting impression on a patient, connecting with him or her on the most personal level, just because I have been that patient.

To all of the PAs at MD Anderson who touched my life, who saved me from death, I am here because of you. I have been involved in health care ever since my diagnosis, and I can firmly say that every day brings a joy to my heart. There are many joys in life, but none such greater than providing joy to others. As a patient, I have seen it all from simple blood draws to near-death situations. None of which would not have been conquered without the presence of my PAs. It is in this life-altering experience I find myself providing the best patient care.

This letter says it all. In spite of his struggle with sustaining his life and dealing with complications, his thoughts were about how he could help others going through the same thing.

Chapter 10

Rakesh wanted to go to India to visit Guru, but it was considered not safe for him to do so. He had increased his normal activities in 2014. On March 19, 2014, he took part in a Relay for Life race in Houston, and he was able to finish and had fun doing so.

He still had to continue his outpatient testing and low-dose chemo at home. At the end of June 2014, he had a setback. His MRD test came back positive, and he had some blast cells only in CSF, as determined by obtaining this fluid through a spinal tap, which he had undergone many times during the last three years, though only at a lower limit during one of his blood tests. They decided to wait and repeat in a few weeks.

During mid-July that same year, Guru was visiting from India and was only going to be in the New York and New Jersey area since he was in his nineties and suffering from strokes along with declining health. Rakesh twisted His Oncologist's arm to let him go to New York to get Guru's blessing in person. And he volunteered in helping in new constructions for the new temple. He did that for three to four days, in spite of his limited strength.

His devotion was his willpower. It was very crowded and dangerous for Rakesh since his immunity was far from adequate. He took precautions by wearing face masks and using antiseptic solution. In spite of a huge crowd of people waiting to pay their respects to Guru, albeit from a distance, Rakesh managed to get close to Guru and pay respect to him by touching Guru's feet. Guru gave him a blessing.

When I heard that, I thought, since Rakesh could not go to India to get Guru's blessing, Guru came in person to do so. Guru had come to the United States for another agenda. But I believe it was completely Rakesh's good karma. Even though Rakesh did not verbalize it, I know he was at peace from that point onwards.

In August, I was in Colorado for my periodic visits during construction of my home. I had promised Rakesh that, when he was completely better, he would come to my home in Colorado, and we could go skiing one more time, as he had expressed his desire to do so.

My niece called me and told me that Rakesh's bone marrow had increased blast cells and MRD was increasing, indicating a relapse of ALL. His spinal fluid also showed blast cells, indicating cancer had spread to the central nervous system.

In the fall of 2014, during a new diagnosis of relapse and before starting radiation treatment, Rakesh said to me one evening in his hospital room, "Dakshafoi, the new iPhone 6 is out."

"Let's just wait until December or so, and then we can get it after all the bugs are worked out in the new system."

"Okay."

Around mid-September, he started radiation treatment for CNS involvement. Ketki and I both hung around an extended time for his first radiation treatment. That evening, we headed back to Dallas, Ketki especially since Amrish and Krishma's wedding was coming up. Papaji and Naliba once again took over the task of taking him three times a week for radiation at MDA. I had to work the two weekends.

October 11 was Amrish and Krishma's wedding. I had to work the first weekend of October. I went straight from work to Houston on October 6 to take over help with radiation treatment, while the grandparents headed over the same afternoon to Dallas to help with wedding arrangements and various events prior to the ceremony.

By that time, Rakesh had twisted the radiation physician's arm to let him have treatments on Saturdays as well. So he had only two treatments left, one on October 7 and the last on October 8. He was very sick from it, but he did not show it. He could hardly drink, let alone eat. We had planned to leave for Dallas on October 9, two days before the wedding.

On October 8, when we were going for the last treatment, there was an accident on the highway we were to go through, and it was completely shut down. And it was thirty minutes before we found a way to turn around and take an alternate route, which was longer. We reached the facility about forty-five minutes late. But he received treatment soon after we got there.

After that, he wanted to leave for Dallas the same day. He made me call Amrish, the pharmacist, to get magic mouthwash mixture ingredients so I could call it in at the pharmacy in Dallas for him to have it for relief of sore throat. He had so much faith in his brother that he would not let me alter it to make it better. He wanted to surprise his parents and family, so we were not to say anything on the phone when we talked to them after the treatment.

But a little later, Naliba called and told me that we were to give a ride to one of the friends from Houston who was attending the wedding. At that time, we were in dilemma. What to do? We were leaving one day earlier. We had to tell them that we were coming on that day and not the next, thus spoiling the surprise.

The friend did not mind coming one day early. She met us at the temple. We also had to pick a garland made of red roses, which saints at the temple had blessed for Amrish to wear during wedding ceremony.

On the way to Dallas, even though he was not feeling well, Rakesh had prolonged conversations with the friend, who was his grandma's age, until we reached home about four and a half hours later. Moreover, I was very surprised that he was talking to her about various people they knew at the temple of all ages, from little kids to the elderly. His knowledge of those people was something beyond my comprehension. He had never talked to me that much when riding with me or other family members in the car. I can only guess that he thought it was his obligation to talk to her so she did not feel out of place. That was the level of consideration for people he had. Ketki was feeling beyond joy for having her baby home for the occasion.

I am sure the next three to four days were very stressful for him. His throat was not any better. I think the magic mouthwash might have helped him little. He did not want to miss any of the festivities before the wedding.

Culturally weddings tend to be very hectic, not to mention stressful. Rakesh was determined to enjoy and participate in all of the activities. He did not want to miss even a second of his brother's wedding. I think he was the happiest person, next to the bride and groom. The best moments were that he drove his brother to the wedding site in the rented Maserati convertible. The temperature outside was on cooler side. But he did not seem to mind it. I think, deep inside, he knew that this might be the last time he would be with his brother and family.

One of the traditions is that the groom and friends dance in the street outside the wedding facility. As much as Rakesh loved to dance, he had no strength. But he danced his last dance, albeit for a few seconds, with his brother.

He sat next to his brother at the altar for the entire ceremony, which took about four hours or so. And then at the reception, he gave the best man speech. He was funny. He joked about childhood incidents. At the same time, he was sentimental. At the end of speech, he thanked his parents for a lifetime of love and comfort. People in attendance laughed and cried at the same time.

Chapter 11

After radiation, he was declared cancer free. Since he had relapsed within three years of his original diagnosis, he was considered at high risk for relapse again. And chances of survival would be 22 percent. With transplant, the chance for survival would increase to 50 percent.

Before his brother's wedding, the decision was already made for him to undergo a bone marrow transplant after Amrish was back from his honeymoon. Amrish was to be a donor for that since he was the only match they had until now, though a half match only.

On November 8, 2014, he was admitted to MD Anderson on the pediatric floor since that was the only available room for prepping him to receive a bone marrow transplant. A couple days prior to that, he had gone to the sperm bank for storing his sperm (though probably already damaged) for future use since the heavy-duty chemo he was to receive as preparation for transplant would surely render him sterile. He was started on intense chemo to shut down his bone marrow. It was painful to watch him go through pain, constant hiccups, and tremors.

One day, Rakesh and I were alone in his hospital room, swapping stories. I said, "Hey, Rock, let's get new phones now."

"Let's wait until new year, just in case there are still some bugs."

I was in shock. *Rock wants to wait for a new device? That's not the Rakesh we know.*

In hindsight, he already knew that his end was near. It was not even in the back of my mind. The thought of him not being with us had not even entered in mind. It was not an option.

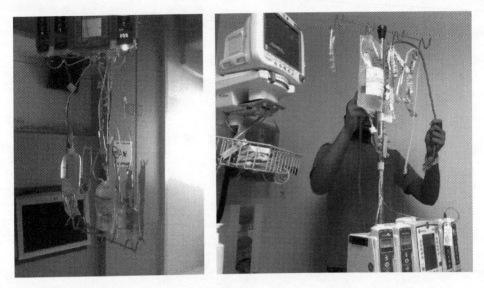

On November 9, 2014, he tweeted, "Butt Kicking day; My decorated IV pole."

On November 16, 2014, he tweeted, "Day before transplant. Sorry fat fingers. The limdi tree in dada khachars darbar has been pruned of extra bags—lol."

He was very sick from the chemo. He was swollen like a toad. The most noticeable problem was continuous hiccups and not to mention severe headaches. But during all these difficult times, he never lost his deep faith in God and Guru. He was miserable but handling them like a trooper.

On November 16, 2014, he tweeted again, "Swami's arshivad once again. He said evertything will be OK. It always is. This mortal body has hard time understanding that.

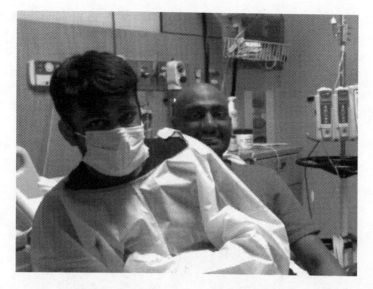

The donner and donee. Ready to kick cancers butt with swamis arshirvad!"

The D-day, November 17, 2014, came. Amrish, his wife, Krishma, and I left for MD Anderson very early in the morning. Amrish had a brief conversation with the doctor about the procedure and answered the questions he, Krishma, or I had. They were to take about a thousand milliliters of bone marrow under general anesthesia.

The procedure went well, though it took close to three hours. Ketki came by at the end of procedure to see her oldest son after the procedure. Ketki and I visited briefly after Amrish was in recovery. After that, we both left for Rakesh's room since his brother's bone marrow was on the way there. Krishma stayed with Amrish.

A few minutes later, Amrish's bone marrow arrived. The transplant doctor came, and it was started. On the outside, it looked just like a blood transfusion he had received hundreds of times in the last three years. All of us stared at the bag on the IV pole containing the bone marrow for several minutes. The doctor left after a few minutes. The nurse stayed in the room to monitor his vital signs and so forth closely. I ate the vanilla ice cream Rakesh had ordered for me from the hospital cafeteria.

A couple hours later, Amrish was discharged. So I went to get him and Krishma. On the way down, I pleaded with a sympathetic face for the transporter to leave us in the lobby and not wait for me to bring the car around since I did want Amrish to visit his brother, look at a bag of his bone marrow, and see Rakesh. The transporter was understanding.

So in a wheelchair, up we went to Rakesh's room. Krishma and I stood outside the room while Amrish put on his gown and mask to go into the room. I can only imagine what the conversation was like. Ketki told me that, when they hugged each other, Rakesh told him, "This is my Superman. Thanks for saving my life."

Both were all smiles.

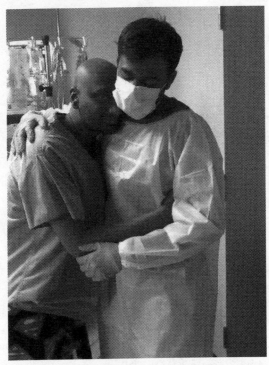

Thanks for Saving My Life

On November 17, 2014, he tweeted, "Wow, what a day Transplant is done. We did good. See for yourself."

Chapter 12

By the second day, Rakesh already was showing severe signs and symptoms of transplant rejection. He was having severe bloody diarrhea and bloody vomiting, not to mention sluffing of his mucous membrane. He could not eat, to say the least. I was very frustrated and upset at hospital system for not providing IV nutrition.

I had to leave to go to work the weekend at Waco on November 27 through November 30. I went back to Houston on December 1. I was getting daily reports from Ketki about the progress. He showed signs of veno-occlusive disease (VOD). She and I discussed during that time about starting him on experimental medicine for VOD. The danger of that drug was internal bleeding, as if he did not have enough of that issue.

Once again, I had to leave for Waco on December 4. From the phone conversation with Ketki, I could sense that her positive attitude was waning, and it seemed like she was at wit's end. I can just imagine being with Rakesh twenty-four hours a day and watching him suffer could get very stressful. I even mentioned that to nurses at Waco.

They said, "It's all right. She needs to not keep all her emotions inside."

On December 6, 2014, he had a collapsing episode while standing with the transporter to go for a CT scan, and they had to call code blue. While code was called, Amrish and his grandparents were at the entrance of the unit. Amrish called his mom, asking jokingly if it were Rakesh.

Ketki said yes. Before she could say anything else, Amrish dropped everything and ran in the unit to Rakesh. CPR was successful. Then he went for the CT scan of his abdomen. Due to this episode, the nurse accompanied him and Ketki, along with the transporter.

On the way, Rakesh was joking with the nurses. "I am going to be a PA, and then I will boss you and other nurses around."

Ketki called me again and told me that he was being moved to ICU for observation. He seemed to be stable at that time. One hour later, she called me and said he was being placed on a ventilator to help him breathe. At that time, Rakesh was very much awake and communicating. Amrish talked to him to make sure Rakesh knew what they were about to do.

I asked if I should come over now. Ketki knew that I did not like to drive in the dark, especially alone. I said I would leave early in the morning to come over.

I called my partner. "Rakesh is in the ICU and on a ventilator, so if come early in the morning, I can leave."

"Why don't you leave now? I can come over now."

"Ketki told me it was not necessary."

I had a hard time going to sleep. Finally I did so after a couple of hours.

Rakesh was paralyzed and heavily sedated in order to ventilate him better. Peritoneal dialysis was also started due to kidney failure.

At around 3:00 a.m. on December 7, his blood pressure was dropping and not responding to multiple medications used to maintain his blood pressure. Ketki started calling family members. Guru was also called for blessing for him so his soul could find his way to heaven. Even though Guru could hardly speak due to stroke, he did this time in a very soft, muffled voice.

Chapter 13

On December 7, 2014, I was in the call room at work, sleeping. At 4:00 a.m., a call came exactly three years after a call from Ketki stating, "Rakesh is in the hospital."

This time, my sister-in-law- Naliba, Rakesh's grandma, said, "Leave now." I jumped out of my bed, desperately packing my suitcase while placing a call to my partner. I rushed in the NICU. I was shaking, and my voice was cracking. Finally I managed to tell the nurses that I must leave right away. I told my partner nothing critical was going on at this moment in the unit.

One of the nurses helped me and carried my suitcase to the car. Early morning, it was still very dark on a chilly December morning. I don't like driving in dark. But at this point, I really did not care. It was a three-hour drive. I kept praying and wishing. I kept asking God to please take my life right now but save Rakesh. I had "been there, seen that, and done that," and Rakesh had his whole life ahead of him.

I said, "He has to be there, see that, and do that. He wants to ski one more time."

When I entered the Houston area, I turned on my flashers so I could get to Rakesh as soon as possible. It was Sunday morning, so there was no traffic to slow me down. When I reached MD Anderson, I did not waste time to park. I just handed over the car to the valet attendant. Since it was the weekend, the security required a driver's license, but I was fumbling to get it out and asked in a cracking voice, "What floor is the ICU, and what elevator to take? My grandson is critical."

The security guard told me how to get there and realized that I was very much in distress, so he let me go without checking my ID. I literally ran to the elevator and the ICU. Ketki was waiting outside for me. We hugged each other, and with tears in her eyes while walking toward Rakesh's room, she said, "Doc, he is not responding."

In the room, Naliba was saying religious mantras to Rakesh, hoping he was hearing that. As I saw Rakesh all swollen up, laying still and hooked up to a ventilator, multiple IVs, and dialysis machine, I could not control myself.

I hugged him. With tears running down, I kept saying, "Rock, beta (son), please don't give up. Don't give up. Try to take some breaths. Fight the machine."

I found out, not only was he heavily sedated, he was also paralyzed. I insisted to the attending doctor to stop the paralyzing medicine so he could breathe. Also he was on multiple medicines to maintain his blood pressure. I was sure that, after he was off the paralyzing medicine, his blood pressure would respond better.

I kept asking him to constantly breathe while hugging him. The family was considering removing life support. I broke down several times in the meantime. When physicians were making rounds, I told them I refused to take him off life support after less than twenty-four hours of trying. They agreed to that. Also they found out that I was a NICU doctor. For the rest of the day, they let me do anything I thought would work.

By midmorning, Rakesh's dad-Bharat, Harshaddada and Sarojba came. They had started from Dallas the same time I had from Waco.

I did not leave his room. The family forced me to eat something. I went into the waiting area for five minutes and drank a half-cup of coffee and two bits of food. And I had to leave when the saints came over from the temple to give Rakesh blessings. For the rest of the day, I sat in a chair in a fetal position and periodically went to Rakesh and kept urging him not to give up and take one breath, just one breath, for me.

After stopping the paralyzing agent, he did take a couple of breaths, but there was no movement or response to touch or voice. Throughout the day, I noticed his blood pressure was very sensitive to the medicines he was getting. If any one of three stopped, his blood pressure would go down. Nurses had to refill those almost every hour.

By the early evening, the rest of the relatives from Florida and New York came as well. All of the immediate family from both maternal and paternal sides was there.

When the night shift came, I asked the nurse, "Why does he not have compression stockings?"

She checked the order and put those on. At that time, I saw him slightly moving the one leg. I thought maybe he would turn around.

I asked the nurse, "I know only one person is allowed to stay in the room, but under no circumstances am I going to leave him. I will sit in the corner behind the pole so no one will see me."

"Okay, but be quiet and not conspicuous so no one knows you are here."

"I promise."

Ketki was contemplating going home since I was staying and she had not slept in over two days.

"You should also stay," I told her.

So she slept behind the pole in a reclining chair. No one could see her. That allowed me to stay by the pole on a chair. I continued to sit in a fetal position. Ketki slept well. I somewhat dozed of for thirty minutes or so at midnight.

The rest of the time, I tried to manage his ventilation according to blood gas results and oxygen saturation monitor. The nurse was also adjusting his dialysis machine. His kidneys were completely shut down, and there was very little urine output. Through the night, his oxygen saturations kept dropping in spite of being 100 percent oxygen. I tried changing the ventilator to see if any of the settings would help.

The nurse and respiratory therapist were nice enough to do whatever I wanted to do. All was in vain, and his oxygen saturations kept going down. Also blood pressures were very unstable and difficult to keep at acceptable levels, in spite of maximum dose of medicines.

Around 5:00 a.m., Ketki heard the nurse and respiratory therapist discussing what was next and woke up frantically. "What's going on?"

"Ketki, he is not responding to anything. I am trying to help. He is not listening to me." She got up and stood by the bed, sad but not saying anything. After a few minutes, she said, "I am going to brush and wash my face."

When outside the room, she called home and told everyone to come. When they got there, without my knowledge, they all, including Ketki, talked outside in waiting area and decided to let him go to God.

Around 7:00 a.m., I saw nurses come over and disconnect everything while Ketki, Bharat, Papaji and Naliba stood there watching. Hareshaddada and Sarojba stood just outside the room. They were all singing the mantra "Swaminaranyan" over and over again. Naliba and Ketki stroked his body. They had to stop since it was interfering with monitoring his heart rate.

I was sitting in my chair, in the same position I had been in for the last twenty-four hours. I was too numb to say or do anything. My tears had dried by now.

Less than fifteen minutes after stopping everything, his heart stopped. Rock was no more. The nurses wanted everyone to wait in waiting area so they could remove all he was attached to. I did not leave. I just sat there, watching, while nurses did whatever they needed to do. I did not leave him alone even for a second, except for a few minutes when the saints came to visit and pray.

After a couple of hours, Ketki and my sister-in-law came to the room to get me. I did not want to leave, but they forced me. We stood outside in the lobby. I still did not want to go. Instead I wanted to go to the morgue with him. Of course that was not an option I had. I waited until transporters came to take him. Then I drove home, along with the rest of the family in their respective cars. naliba rode with me.

Chapter 14

Rakesh's Journey through ALL

The day after he was diagnosed with ALL, he knew he would have to limit visitations from the friends and well-wishers. He also knew that he and his family would be inundated with phone calls. So he started almost daily tweets. Reading those tweets, I was amazed at his strength and resolve. His faith in God and Guru was beyond anyone's imagination. I have cited most important tweets, which I believe are great lessons for anyone one who is going through the similar issues with health. During three years, he never lost his sense of humor and resolve. He was at peace knowing that whatever was happening to him was God's wish.

The tweets I have omitted are mainly what food he ate. Eating is a ritual people take for granted until one cannot eat because of the side effects of chemotherapy. Then any food becomes a great treat. Also he has referred to Amrish at "Bhai" in the tweets- his nick name for brother.

December 9, 2011

Jai Swaminarayan! We will be posting pictures and updates on my health here. Thanks for all the prayers. We will really appreciate it!
I'm doing fine, just had some OJ! It was very refreshing.

December 10, 2011

Finally, with Amrish and Dad. The family is here.
Thanks for your support I love you all.
Just trimmed. Now going to sleep.
Takorji and santos came to visit.

December 12, 2011

No chemo yet. Just waiting for the final word from the pathologist. Had a good day today. Ate well, slept well. **Ready to tackle the world!!!**
New hair style!

December 14, 2011

Good morning all, ALL! Lol. No chemo yet, need results on chromosomes!! Maybe tmr. Just showered! Aaahaa! **Appreciate the prayers! Waiting.**

December 16, 2011

Feeling pretty good right now! Have the worst case of the hiccups! Besides that, nothing major. Eat, sleep and more eat sleep.

December 17, 2011

Ok, so I think the hiccups have stopped for now. Second session of chemo is scheduled for monday. :-).Had chest X-ray. All is well! Gud nite

December 18, 2011

On to another session of chemo tomorrow. Mom gets to be the certified infusion tech. She'll change the dressing on my IV weekly starting tmr
Hello. Today's update, sore throat. It hurts to swallow. Doc Gave me 'magic wash'! It numbs the inside so I can swallow. **watching game**

December 19, 2011

Mom just changed the dressing on the central line nd I'm still alive, lol. Just started chemo, this one is looong, 2 hrs, so nap time. :-)XOX
Done with second round! YEAH! Ate lunch. Just tired nd sleepy. **it's raining, perfect for another nap. Zzzzzz**

December 20, 2011

OMG, going home today. Can't wait. Got my platelets, my drugs. Am ready to GO!! Please no visitors at home!! The infection control police
Are in full swing. Will continue to tweet. **Thank you all for ur support nd prayers.** Home sweet home, here I come

December 21, 2011

Wow, what a day. Outpatient therapy was grueling. My first puke since chemo started on the way back from the clinic. Dehydrated a little.
Didn't make it to the tournament, the gang was kind enough to get me a tee.

December 23, 2011

More puking this morning. Tired and cold. No other issues. **ALL is well, lol.**

December 24, 2011

Had to make a dash to the hospital with shortness of breath nd tightness in the chest. Blood tests, X-rays all look good.
Waiting for doc to say its ok to go home again ... Will b doing quite a bit of that ... it's ALL good. Am resting now, thank to morphin. :-)
Sorry, got home a few hrs ago. Feeling good. Throat still raw but the magic wash will do its thing. Good night all. C u in the am

December 27, 2011

Today is a good day ate pancakes and drinking lots of water. Played UNO with the family last night

December 28, 2011

At the hospital ready for another dose of chemo
Waiting at the hospital bored out of my mind.
Man what a crazy day 1 bag of platelets, 2 bags of blood, 2 different chemo drugs, and a bone marrow aspiration. **Still standing all is good**

December 30, 2011

Day 16: Blast cells down to 16%. **Jumping with joy.**

January 2, 2012

ALL is good. Blood is doing good too. No problems today, just wanna eat queso, hummus, had a dream that my ba made 8 course punjabi meal!
My daddy nd bhai went back to Dallas:-(. My foiba also went back :-(. Long day today. Had blood work at 7:40 AM!! Was home by 11:00 :-).
Meditating, lol

January 4, 2012

Blood count is borderline. Will need to come back on Saturday for a recheck. Chemo # 4 almost done. The cool aid just started. Yum!!
So we're back! The weakness got worst so we came in for some hot chocolate,
M D A Style!!! Lol!! (*photo*)

January 5, 2012

Not a good day today. Feel blah and cranky. Gud luck to my bhai for his surgery tomorrow. **Going to have to share all the attention w/him:-)**

January 6, 2012

Well, bhais surgery went well, he's home resting. **So I thought it would be a good idea to come visit the Leukemia center, lol. Liked the hot chocolate so much, we decided to stay the night.** Heart rate is too high and cardiac enzymes are not normal, lol. Running test.

So much for bhai getting all the attention. He's doing good so I guess it's ok. Mom can hardly keep her eyes open. I should let her sleep?

January 9, 2012

Bone marrow aspiration #2 complete!!

We're looking for less than 5% blast cells! Fingers are crossed **Bapas in mind! :)**

Hello, maybe be going home today. Things are progressing. Tolerated soup and crackers. **Heart monitor is unplugged so rate must b gud. :-)**

Finally back home! :)

January 10, 2012

Good day today! Chemo and spinal tap tomorrow! :0 **Tomorrow is also blast cell count day!!! Wohooo!**

January 11, 2012

Blast count. Wait for it **... 2%!!!** **Houston, we are in remission!!** Off to get my spinal tap and chemo!!

January 12, 2012

Yet another great day!! And many more to come!! :)

January 13, 2012

Sarangpur, here I come, NOT!!! Like my newest look?? My bhai gave it to me. Having an ok day. Bones ache. **ALL is gud**

January 17, 2012

Samosas and spring rolls … good combination.
Great day today!!! :)
Starting cycle 2 tomorrow!!! Bring it on!!!

January 18, 2012

Well, no chemo today!! Waiting for counts to get a little bit higher … On my way home :)

January 19, 2012

Too many potatoes today!!!!!
Hopefully cycle two starts tomorrow!!
I'm ready for it to get started!!! Woot woot!! :)

January 20, 2012

ANC count is still not where the doc wants it. Chemo will resume next Friday the 27th. I get the week off!! **Wohooo :)**

January 26, 2012

I got tendonitis :(
Sad news: bhai left today. Good news: went for a walk, **feels good to get some fresh air**

February 3, 2012

Ready for the superbowl!!!

February 15, 2012

Not doing that well. Headache is still there and not able to do anything except lay in bed and sleep.
Finally sat down to eat.

February 27, 2012

Well, that didn't last long. We're back in the hospital with fever and headaches again. Had to take hydromorphine for the pain. Waiting ...

February 29, 2012

Back home again! Hopefully, for a while. ALL is well. No fever, no headache, just a little neuropathy in the feet. Ready for more chemo!

March 5, 2012

Phase 2 starts today! Going to receive a cocktail of chemo! Feeling great!

March 6, 2012

Neurologist appointment today! Going to get to the bottom of these crazy headaches!! :)

March 7, 2012

Been a good day. Tired for the most part, but **all** is well! Goodnight!! :)

March 19, 2012

At the hospital for blood work and then therapy. Going to be a long day!!

March 23, 2012

My bad for not tweeting in a while. Will try to get caught up today and stay caught up. Forgot to tell all that bhai is in town. :):):):). Monday's therapy was looong. Had an allergic reaction to chemo and platelets. ODed on benedryl. Bhai took good care of me. Lol. Yesterday was a good day. Today, blood work. Hopefully, will not need a transfusion. Wish bhai could stay for a while. :(he'll be back :) Tuesday was good, just tiring. Spent a lot of quality time with my bhai. Had pain puri, sevpuri for dinner. :) tendinitis is still there. Wednesday, woke up with a headache. But it was gone after breakfast. Took it easy for the rest of the day. Dal, bhaat, shaak for dinner.

March 25, 2012

Well, Friday turned out to be a long day. Got two bags of blood. Had pizza for an early dinner. Sat had taco pizza. Today am just tired.

April 1, 2012

Happy birthday to maharaj!!
Just got back from aarti. Feeling great!

April 3, 2012

Spiked a fever this morning (102)
In the ER waiting to be admitted to the hospital. Hopefully it's not a long stay! :)

April 4, 2012

Fever stayed high throughout the night, but has finally come down now. Waiting for the blood cultures to grow! Wait wait wait!
Mom and docfoi came, :) down for ct of sinus, lol. What do they expect to find in there? B/c headache is behind the eyes, doc wants to check

April 5, 2012

Feeling good, just no appetite. But am eating a little. CT was normal. Duh! Waiting for cultures to grow, lol. Hopefully tomorrow. :):):):)

April 6, 2012

Ready to go home! Had my bone marrow aspiration, got my dressing changed, loaded up with IV antibiotics. wore out.

April 7, 2012

Good dinner, chole bhature! Mmmmm! Feeling a little better. Still a little tired. BUT, **this too shall pass.**
Still very tired. Just had bkfst and lunch together. Not feeling bad but not feeling good either. **Just blah!! This too shall pass!!** :)

April 10, 2012

Hi all. Doing ok. Went for a walk with my grandpa yesterday. Ended up with leg cramps!! will try again. :)

April 13, 2012

Bring it on. Am so ready for the next cycle to start. It's like waiting for Xmas, lol checking out the orders.

April 14, 2012

What a day yesterday. Consolidation two has begun!! Feeling the effects today. Body hurts, hair (whats left) hurts. But overall, doing good.

April 16, 2012

Had meeting with transplant team. Will need bone marrow transplant. Yeepee! ALL is well. Still feel week from chemo. Blood work is good.

April 18, 2012

Mom and dad left yesterday:(hanging out with baa and dada. :) feeling pretty good today. Had lasagna for dinner, yum. Docfoi made it :)

April 23, 2012

Blood work then chemo. All is well!

April 27, 2012

Chimmichangas for lunch!! Compliments of pinkyben!!! They were awesome!! :)
At MDA for blood work and dressing change. Mom and dad are coming today!! Wohoo! Feeling great! Got to go to mandir today to do the Darshan of many santos. **What a great day it has been!! :)**

April 29, 2012

Great 21st bday! Got to catch up with some amazing friends! Ate some great food! **Love all of y'all!! Thanks for the great day!!!**

May 2, 2012

Been a great week thus far! Trying to fatten up before the transplant!! Haha

May 8, 2012

Been nauseated for the past couple of days with stomach pains. Feeling better today though :)

May 14, 2012

Blood work at MDA. Been feeling a bit queazy for the past couple of days, but feelings a bit better today

At the clinic for blood work, meeting with college rep, transplant doc and chemo. Tired already. Everyone, pls sign up for marrow donor. And encourage all ur friends and family members to do so as well. At http://bethematch.com. It's easy and it could save a life, maybe mine.

June 2, 2012

Went to rajipo din today for a bit, was fun! Been feeling fairly well for the past couple of weeks. Start up cycle three Wednesday!!!

June 8, 2012

Cycle 3 was postponed due to low white cell count ... Looking to start for sure next Friday!! I get a whole week off from hospital! Party! :)

June 15, 2012

Party's over? Hardly! Consolidation 3 has begun!!! Finally. New drugs are being introduced. Sure they will fair well.

June 16, 2012

Chemo went well. Just really really tired as want to sleep all day haha

June 29, 2012

Back in Houston for chemo! Been doing well!!
Chemo went well today!! Had it in me to have some pasta. :)

June 30, 2012

Too many potatoes today!! Post chemo day, no complications! Just feeling a bit groggy. **All is well**

July 2, 2012

Feeling a bit moppy and groggy today. Chemo is kicking in little late. All is well!
Had marble slab with my mommy :)

July 6, 2012

Blood counts looking good!! Starting chemo next Friday!! :)
Kofta and naan :)
Cadbury ice cream bar :) good way to end the night :)

July 10, 2012

Good day!! Out for a walk! :)
Walked 1.05 miles!! most exercise I've done in the past 7 months!!
Feels great!!! :)

July 13, 2012

exercising—feel exhausted now!!! I just finished a 1.21 mi run with Nike+ Running.
Hospital day!! Start consolidation 3b today!!! Chemo chemo chemo!
Big bad of fluids!!! Ima be peeing all freaking night!!!!
Back home! Chemo was difficult, but pulled through it! Ready to eat :)

July 20, 2012

At MDA, no chemo!!! Just a lumbar puncture!! :) playing the waiting game

July 23, 2012

Return of the headaches part II!!! Headaches are back, little bit milder than last time though. At MDA for blood work and dressing change!:)

July 25, 2012

Had to pay a visit to the ER last night. 102 degree fever!!! Waiting for blood cultures to grow. Head is pounding!!! Long night!!

July 26, 2012

Ended up staying. Still spiking fever and headaches are getting worst. Doc ordered ct scan. Waiting ...

July 28, 2012

Still have low grade fever, headache is down to a 3-4. More chemo today, it's the one that causes problems, good thing I'm in the hospital.

August 1, 2012.

Wow, what a week. Was going to go home Monday, instead ended up in ICU Sunday night. Pretty spooky, couldn't move my right leg and left arm
Then couldn't think straight, could not walk. The final word, it's TIA. Mini stroke but very temporary. Can walk/talk just fine. :-)

August 4, 2012

A first for me, at the clinic on a saturday for blood work. ALL is well, just need potassium. Waiting game is the same as any other day.

August 9, 2012

Been doing well for the past couple of days! Slowly gaining strength back!

August 10, 2012

At MDA getting a bone marrow aspiration today! Need this one to be MRD(minimal residual disease) negative, so I can continue my treatment!!

August 17, 2012

Biopsy results are back and ... MRD is NEGATIVE!!! :) no transplant!!! Wohooo!!! All else is well!! Thanks for all the prayers! :)

August 24, 2012

At the clinic to start new cycle. It's going to be a loooong day. But Maharaj and swami will be halp make it shorter. Mom nd dad r here:-)

August 27, 2012

Hello. Ended up in the hospital again Saturday night. Fever, headache, vomiting, lol. That's what I get for taking a chemo cocktail, haha.

August 31, 2012

At MDA for blood work! **All** is going well since my discharge from the hospital :)

September 10, 2012

At MDA again for blood work and review!! I've been doing really well past couple of days!! Walked almost 2 miles the other day!! :)

September 16, 2012

Enjoying some Sunday football! Feeling good!! :)

September 19, 2012

Went to shayan aarti today and got to catch up with the santos! All in all, it's been a good day! Just feeling a tad bit tired! :)

September 23, 2012

Had a visit from P. Amrutnandan Swami and P. Aksharmurti Swami! Felt great to do sant samagam! :)
Sunday=football day :) feeling great!!!

September 25, 2012

Post chemo: Got home at 10:30 last night. Feeling super drained today, and mood less!! Just relaxing today and keeping hydrated!!!

September 26, 2012

Back in the hospital. Spiked a fever at 2 AM. Doctor doesn't know the cause f the fever just yet. Big time headache and fever still there

September 28, 2012

No fever for 24 hrs. If it stays that way for another 24 hrs, I can go home tomorrow. Feeling GREAT!

September 29, 2012

Back home!! Feeling great!! :)

September 30, 2012

No place like home. Pic taken in the hospital
Yeah, NO PLACE LIKE HOME!!

October 5, 2012

At MDA getting blood work done, and then chemo time!! Feeling good, just been feeling heavy in the stomach. **All is well** :)

October 9, 2012

At MDA for my last chemo of the month!!! Starting the steroids back up today! Feeling well!!! :)

October 29, 2012

At MDA again. Kinda bummed. No chemo today, schedule mess up. Will get PEG on on Wednesday. Just a little tired. Not too bad.

October 21, 2012

FOOTBALL SUNDAY!!! Feeling great!! :)

October 31, 2012

Waiting at MDA for chemo ... Feeling good. Started taking steroids this cycle, making me feel heavy in the stomach, but **all is well!** :)

November 2, 2012

At MDA for some chemo!! One week break from the steroids!! Feeling well, just a bit tired!! **All is well** :)
Minimal residual disease is still a negative!! Great news!! On the right path for recovery!! Best news all day! :)

November 19, 2012

First time in a year ALL my counts are in the "normal" range!! :)
Feeling great!! Feels good to be back home!!

November 30, 2012

Back in Houston, at MDA ready to start my LAST cycle of chemo!! :)

December 4, 2012

Been in the hospital since Sunday. Hopefully, last night!
Celebrating!

December 21, 2012

Let the countdown begin. At the clinic for my LAST chemo.
All done!
(Photo-with last chemo sign)

August 13, 2013

Looks like the results from my latest bone marrow came back.
STILL CANCER FREE, **all thanks to Maharaj and Swami!
Blessed to have them!** :)

November 8, 2014

Today we start yet another journey towards kicking cancers butt!
30 days in the 'resort'. Not bad.

November 9, 2014

Butt kicking -Day. My decorated IV pole.
TV Commercial - AT&T Network Experts: "Third Party"
Ending day one with some laughs and football.
cancer=cancel. Yummy cupcake! Tomorrow 6:00 am chemo.

November 10, 2014

Morning tea has been served on the dot at 6:00am. PK levels
checked 5 times. Oh yes, and my new friend to check PK levels
My new friend. *(photo of line)*

November 11, 2014

Had a bit of nausea and vomiting this morning, coupled with slight headache. Other than that, feeling great!! Dad is here!!! Wohoooooo!
Ending the day with a HUGE headache!
Had to take to stop theIng. Tomorrow chemo at 5:00 am and 6:00am. Good night all.

November 12, 2014

T-5 days. Doing as well as can be expected. Platelets Headaches, chills, nausea, weakness Maharaj and swami will provide strength

November 13, 2014

But tomorrow is a new day and swami give the strength to kick cancers butt.
T-4 and counting. It has been a looong day.
Mom's back, tremors started yesterday and are getting worst. Can't even take meds w/o help.

November 14, 2014

T-3 days. Last day for chemo. Sat & sun are rest days. Tremors continue, arms & legs cramping, HUGE headache. Otherwise doing GREAT!

November 15, 2014

T-2 days! Rest day. Tremors not too bad. Water retention, joints aching. Goal is to walk 3 times, eat and keep it down. Off to a good start
Not bad if I do say so myself. Didn't quite make this one but made the next one.
(photo basketball)

November 16, 2014

T-1 day! Enjoy the good days while you can. Yesterday took a turn in the evening. Night wasn't much better. WBC is at 0. Ready for tomorrow.

Ready for the BIG day tomorrow. The limdi tree in Dada khacher na darbar

Swami's ashirvad has arrived once again. He said everything will be ok. It always is. This mortal body has a hard time understanding that.

Sorry fat fingers. The limdi tree in dada khachars darbar has been pruned of the extra bags, lol.

The donor and the donee. Ready to kick cancers bit with Swamis aashirvad!

(photo)

November 17, 2014

Rakesh is being premedicated to receive the marrow.

Transfusion started at 12:15. Expected to last for 3-4 hrs. Rakesh is doing well, resting. So far no reaction. BP is good

Swami aashirvad are with us as we move forward. Amrish is in recovery and doing well. They took just a little over a liter.

Wow, what a day! Transplant is done. We did good. See for yourself.

November 19, 2014

A dressing change. Not due until tomorrow but is a bit sore so might as well change it. All normal side effects of transplant process ...

Day +2. Transplant was pretty boring. Day 1 ended with a fever, day 2 started with mucositis (blood in vomit). Hehe. And will end with ...

Swami ni daya thi, all will be good in no time. Tomorrow is another day.

Benefits of pedi floor. Childhood memories. Stomach is really upset. Can't eat, clinical nurse lead got this for me.

November 20, 2014

Day +3 is almost over. May have spent more time on the toilet and over the sink today than in bed. And three days of non-stop hiccups ...
Benefits of pedi floor. Childhood memories. Stomach is really upset. Can't eat, clinical nurse lead got this for me.
Ending the day with a fever and severe pain from the hiccups.

November 21, 2014

Day+4. No fever less vomiting and diarrhea. Hiccups still continue. New on the menu, double and blurry vision. Had a couple of ct scans
According to the doctor, I'm ahead of the curve, post transplant.
Maharaj and Swami ni keupa Che, Che ne Chej

November 22, 2014

Day +5. Anti rejection drugs! Yummy. Feeling crummy. Blurry vision getting worse. Waiting for doc to order MRId

November 23, 2014

Mom and dad trade places today. Feeling very tired. Diarrhea still bad. Mouth sores are BAD. Making a meal out of ice chips.

November 27, 2014

Day +10. A lot to be thankful about. Maharaj and swami are always with us. A little swelling on the feet.

November 28, 2014

Awesome well-wishers! Thank you, Neil, Neelam, Meghan and Sohil.
(2 photos)

November 29, 2014

Day +12. Happy birthday BAPA! Doing well. Diarrhea and vomiting getting better. swelling and rash getting worst. something new everyday.

November 30, 2014

Day+13. Had a CT & MRI of brain. Am delusional, VERY jittery, talking even when I'm awake. Side effect of meds. Maharaj & Swamis lila.

December 1, 2014

Day+14. 2 weeks ago, bhai and I bonded!! Now we're waiting for white blood cells to go up. Shooting for end of the week. CT and MRI normal

December 4, 2014

Day+17. Last 2 day have not been good. Mostly sleeping. Walked a little yesterday. Today, can't keep eyes open. Issues w/ liver & kidneys

Chapter 15

A fter coming home, people were gathering. I did not feel like talking or listening to anyone. I just kept to myself. By the afternoon, I could see the feeling of relief on Ketki's face. In the afternoon, I went to the temple and cried while I was praying in front of God. The next few days, including the day of the funeral, I just kept going to the temple, seeking solitude, since the house was full of friends and relatives.

The temple was nice enough to cook all three meals for whatever number of people was visiting us until the day of funeral, which was three days later.

His Funeral

Hundreds of friends, relatives, and well-wishers came by car pool, bus, and airplane from around the United States and Texas. The temple had arranged for the visitors to go by bus from the temple to the funeral home. Nurses and PAs also came to pay their respects. Alexis, the PA whom Rakesh was very close to, had a hospital badge made with Rakesh's name and PA behind it. She pinned that on Rakesh's shirt, along with her name tag on Rakesh's shirt. People talked about how he had touched their lives, kept them from choosing a wrong path, and held our hands and gave hugs when they needed it the most.

Rakesh had touched many people, even though he had not met them. For the funeral, Ketki's entire IBM office staff and her previous Pepsi director all carpooled and went to Houston. At that time, they told Ketki that, ever since they heard the news, they had been huddling and praying every two hours in the office for two days until they left for Houston.

I did not go to the funeral. I did not want to see his lifeless body. Instead I chose to go to the temple, where I could see him next to God. I prayed and cried my heart out. I found him closer to me at the temple. On the way, I saw an AT&T store and started crying.

I called Ketki at the funeral. "Ketki, he knew. He knew."

Ketki did not say anything, and we both hung up.

Chapter 16

Who Knew?

Several people spoke at the funeral. Saints from the temple also spoke.

Rakesh had such a deep understanding and faith that they had personal experience with him. During weekly assembly, he would frequently lecture the younger children. He frequently talked about *maya* (attachment). His way for developing detachment was to write down on a piece of paper, "Maya," and then throw away or burn that paper. His understanding of life and faith was beyond his age. Saint said "sometimes even we wanted to sit in during his lecture".

Imagine that! A saint, a highly learned being who has mastered Hindu philosophy, thought that he could learn from Rakesh's lecture.

Also his generous and sympathetic nature, which I had observed during his childhood, continued all of his young life. One of his classmates and member of Rass team, Nikita, told a story about his kind nature.

"On Diwali (a Hindu festival equivalent to Christmas for Christians), my parents were out of town. They had a tradition of eating a certain Indian snack called "Tikhi Puri" with chai. I was sad because my parents were out of town for work and they were not there to do that. Rakesh had Naliba make that and brought that to me, along with chai. He spent time with me, and we ate that together. I was so grateful that he did that, in spite of him having to be at the temple to help out in some festivities planned that day."

This seems very trivial, but to Nikita, one who was missing her parents, it was a huge favor and generosity. There were many more who told similar stories, which I missed, and family in grieving status cannot recall all of them at this time. His friends were so sad for his departure that it seemed impossible to relive their experiences with Rakesh.

In addition to many attending the funeral from his college, the student body had a separate memorial at the university two days later. At the memorial in Dallas about a week later, his high school friends from five to six years ago attended the memorial. Such a popularity at such a young age is beyond comprehension.

An article was published in a North American youth newsletter, published by Hindu-BAPS Temple, outlining his journey through ALL. The last paragraph said it all,

> Rakeshbhai was ever-smiling, carefree, and charismatic. He was able to inspire all who had the pleasure of his acquaintance. Strength like that of Rakeshbhai's is not something that is natural because it is something he learned from swamishri (Guru). Throughout his entire endeavor, Rakeshbhai continually said, "One thing I have learned through this is that maharaj (God) and Swami (Guru) will always have your back." Rakeshbhai truly was the personification of someone who had complete trust and conviction in Maharaj and Swami.

Three days later, the family went to see the primary oncologist. Alexis and the research assistant, Kirk, were there as well. After the funeral, my brother asked Alexis, "What did you see in Rakesh or how he affected you so deeply?"

Alexis replied, **"You did not know him."**

That said it all. In preparation for this book, I arranged to meet with his primary oncologist about three years later. The primary oncologist said at the meeting, "During all these years of practice, normally I don't meet with the family in this situation. But my innermost being told me that I needed to meet with Rakesh's family. He moved me as well. Rakesh and I had discussed writing a book about his experience. Whenever we had some bad news to tell him and entered his room, not knowing how to tell that to Rakesh, his smiling face always solved that dilemma."

I asked, "I heard that you were encouraging Rakesh to write a book. What did you want him to write about?"

His emotional status is hard to describe in words. He was sad but joyous, as well as proud and grateful.

"All these years of practice, I have not seen a patient like Rakesh. ADL—adolescent young with leukemia—Rakesh was special and unique. Compared to other patients, he had an unbelievably cool side and strength. He was a pleasure to be around. He always smiled even when not feeling well and hardly could open his mouth. For a young person, he was very compliant. I never had to worry about him not following instructions to the T. He was honest and had wisdom beyond his age. He was a saintly soul. I wanted him to write a book about being a cancer patient and the coping and wisdom he had."

He paused for moment of reflection and added, "We crossed paths for a purpose. Rakesh talked about his deep faith in God and Guru often. A young guy with leukemia wanted to go to New Jersey in August 2014, not only to get blessings from Guru but also to volunteer lifting bricks for building of the new temple, for which Guru was visiting the United States."

Watching the doctor, it was evident that he was amazed in disbelief that a young man barely past adolescence and obviously not feeling well with news of possible relapse was willing to volunteer doing hard, physical work.

We talked about Rakesh deciding to become a PA. He said, "Once he decided to be a PA, Rakesh accelerated his affords toward that goal in spite of physical discomfort. He wanted to help other people since Rakesh had been in their shoes. Rakesh did a shadow internship in the lymphoma clinic instead of the leukemia unit because of HIPAA regulations."

Then he added, "Rakesh was taking care of us. (This includes not only medical staff, but also family.) According to him, when there were bad lab results or news, they were not sure how to approach Rakesh, how we would give him this news, and how to handle their emotions and disappointments. When they entered Rakesh's room, looking at his smiling face, all concerns about how to tell him the results vanished. Rakesh's smile provided them with courage and reassurance."

Then Kurt, the research assistant, added, "No matter how sick Rakesh was, he always smiled. He had a smart brain, but was humble. Rakesh had given me an elephant statue at the time of the birth of my son."

During a recent communication, he mentioned how his son and he were talking about that elephant.

His oncologist expressed the same sentiment as well. Then the doctor pointed to the Apple Award, which Rakesh had recommended him for. He was very emotional reading that to me and said with a choked-up voice,

"Imagine Rakesh was asking me to recommend him for PA admission while he recommended me for this award." The award read as following,

> The Apple Award   9/16/2012
> To: My Oncologist
> From: Rakesh Patel (RP)
> Comments: Thanks for the crash course in blood cancer. Couldn't have asked for better teacher and more importantly for being a best doctor anyone could ask for.
>
>   Rocky☺

He was also amazed when we told him about the late evening at Rakesh's brother's wedding and the best man speech he delivered just two days after he had finished radiation treatment. He was obviously not feeling well. He could not swallow or eat, and he was weak overall.

After the meeting ended, we decided to visit people at the clinic. We met with the nurse assistant in the leukemia clinic. She said about Rakesh, "Beautiful soul. If someone tells you that you have cancer, you drop dead or survive. Even if he is not with us, he was a survivor. He was our baby."

I asked Alexis, the PA who was very close to Rakesh, "What was it that we did not know about Rakesh?"

In response, she sent me a letter.

> My name is Alexis Geppner, and I am a physician assistant in the Leukemia Department at MD Anderson Cancer Center. I first met Rakesh Patel in September 2012, about nine months after he was transferred to MD Anderson Cancer Center following a life-changing diagnosis of leukemia. He was forced to put his studies on hold at the University of Houston where he majored in management information systems and begin the fight of his life.
>
> My first encounter with Rakesh occurred when I helped perform his lumbar puncture, often called a "spinal tap." During this procedure, a very thin needle is inserted into the space between two of the vertebral bones (usually L3-L4 or L4-L5), and spinal fluid is removed for testing. Following collection of the spinal fluid, chemotherapy is injected through the same needle into the canal surrounding the spinal cord to prevent (or treat) leukemia from invading the central nervous system. Many patients are quite

anxious about this procedure; however, Rakesh continued to focus on the goal at hand. He knew it was something he needed to do to get better and was part of the overall plan.

Rakesh and I always had a routine together and often continued the conversation from where we left off the last time. Lumbar punctures aren't particularly enjoyable, but we always tried to make it as painless as possible, and I thoroughly enjoyed spending time with Rakesh. The time spent with him during his procedures was a time where we were able to talk and connect. He was able to share the things he strove for in life and the goals he set for himself. We didn't always talk about treatment, side effects, and test results.

Since we both are from New York, Rakesh and I often reminisced about where we lived, our (terrible) sports teams, and the last time we went back to visit. We mostly talked about the Knicks, whom I hadn't followed much since my heartbreak in 1996, so he was much more "in tune" to the most recent drafts, schedule, and (losing) record. We talked about playing basketball, our positions, and our toughest games. I would often tell him how difficult it was getting back into full-court basketball after being "out of the game" competitively for so long. He would often use basketball as a way to determine whether something was "not right." If he were unable to run down the court due to shortness of breath, he knew he needed to come in for a checkup. (He also teased me about my NY Jets, along with most everyone else in Texas. I wasn't very good at convincing him to root for the Jets.)

While we always had fun talking about our likes and dislikes, Rakesh's questions and topics focused mostly on learning about medicine and the physician assistant profession. As I described initially, Rakesh was enrolled at the University of Houston where he majored in management information systems. Immediately following his induction course of chemotherapy, his interests began to change. Since the day I met Rakesh, he started to hint at his interest in the PA profession. Not long afterward, he decided he wanted to change his career focus and enroll in PA school as soon as his treatment was completed. He began researching the classes he needed to take to get into PA school early on as well as the experience he needed to become a good candidate. Since that day, his interest never ceased.

While receiving chemotherapy, he continued to ask intelligent questions and research the profession. In between his cycles of chemotherapy, Rakesh attended classes to better himself as a candidate for admission into PA school. Even in the midst of intensive chemotherapy, Rakesh was seen in his hospital bed, studying and researching. I remember seeing huge textbooks next to him on his hospital bed. He would tell me, "Oh, I'm just studying for an exam. No big deal," with one arm connected to his chemotherapy.

One day, Rakesh approached me about a PA shadowing opportunity in leukemia. Unfortunately, due to HIPAA violations, he was not permitted to shadow in the same department he was receiving treatment. Refusing to give up on his opportunity to learn more about the profession, Rakesh looked into other departments for shadowing opportunities. Given the knowledge he already obtained as a patient at MD Anderson and his internal drive, I knew Rakesh would succeed.

Once healthy and stable enough to return to school, Rakesh began shadowing in our lymphoma department. He was able to learn and witness firsthand the responsibilities of a physician assistant, including one-on-one visits with patients, physical exams, interpretation of laboratory values, radiological studies, and treatment plans. He was able to sympathize with the patients in a way only someone who had been through it could. He would tell me often how amazing it was to be on the "other side" of cancer where he could actively help someone else with this terrible disease.

Rakesh remained focused, driven, and extremely responsible prior to, during, and following his diagnosis of leukemia. I always felt his unique knowledge of medicine in the perspective of a patient would have been an essential asset to the physician assistant profession as a clinician. He developed a real passion for the profession with inspiring determination in his will to continue learning despite his circumstances. He never let his disease get in the way of his goals.

Even during the last moments of his life on earth, Rakesh stared fear in the eyes and conquered it with courage and strength. Each battle he took on as a challenge with everlasting determination and never ceased at setting the bar high. I know he is in Akshardham now, fulfilling all that he planned to do on earth. He is still learning and caring for others. We may not be able to witness this with our own eyes, but we can feel it within our hearts. Rakesh is—and will always be—an honorary PA with a cape on his back and a shield on his chest. He will forever be our SUPERMAN.

Reading in between lines in this letter, his generosity and kindness, along with concern for others, in midst of his pain and suffering was evident. How Alexis and Rakesh comforted each other by talking about, not diseases and pain, but sports and other life's pleasures. They did not dwell on what was going on in both their lives. This was very apparent in his personal statement he wrote for application to PA school—how he kept on the path he wanted to take, not thinking and dwelling on his own problem.

Watching him in his room, in darkness, on his computer or phone, I was worried about him developing depression. I was so wrong. He was doing what he had done all of his life, supporting and helping others and staying on that course. Alexis had personal experiences with him, which all of us in the family missed.

Alexis was right. "We did not know him."

His Rass team co-captain, Shreya, told me,

Rakesh was great help in my studies as well. Even though our paths were different (as she was a biology major), I always turned to Rakesh whenever I was feeling anxious and uncertain about my studies. He always managed to calm me and give me confidence and encouragement. And tell me, "Don't worry about anything. Just dance."

According to her, he was the reason she was able to focus, progress, and enroll in medical school. Even after getting admission in medical school about eighteen months later, she looked to him for encouragement.

And Rakesh was always there for her, even when he was going through chemotherapy and dealing with complications.

A tweet from Nikita on December 8, 2014, the day after, read, "You were an amazing friend and even better human being. You will be always remembered and my thoughts."

Finally it seems that Rakesh is communicating with his parents, letting them know that he is okay and saying thanks for love he received. For example, a few months after in late winter, Ketki was feeling down one day. She grabbed a sweater before heading out the door to work. After parking her car, she put on the sweater and started walking toward the building. All of a sudden, she felt a hug, and then she felt a lot better. She was wearing Rakesh's sweater.

Chapter 17

Final Journey

Rakesh's mortal body was not there anymore. Only the ashes were left. His final journey began in the country where he was born and raised. On a bright sunny day, Bharat and Amrish deposited a portion of his ashes in the river. Ketki and other extended family members were standing by the riverbank, watching him on his final journey and praying for his blessed soul. The actual journey began in India three months later.

For a final good-bye, Ketki, Bharat, Amrish, and Rakesh's uncle traveled to India with his ashes to be deposited in the holy river for the final blessing. No, he did not need blessing. He was the blessing. His beloved Guru, Brahm Swaroop Pramukh Sawmi Maharaj, had made sure that he would be at his side eternally.

Father and brother were at the riverbank in long, cotton, white shirts and pants fluttering with the wind. With hands joined in prayer, facing the blinding sun, they quietly stood as Rakesh began the journey down the river, dancing and rejoicing toward the place unknown to us all. For Rakesh, it was just the beginning of the journey down the river, dancing with the waves, toward *Moksha* (liberation), where he hoped to be.

Final Goodbye— Amrish and Bharat

He lived a saint's life in the middle of society and community. He chose to be quiet, spoke few words, and did not tell a soul about how he was helping others. He lived and worked constantly according to Guru's teachings and deep faith in him and God. His visit to New York/New Jersey is the example of it. Even though he knew that he could die from the disease or transplant, he never showed anxiety or left his sense of humor. He managed his pain without heavy-duty medications as long as he could. Only his faith in God allowed him to do so.

It has been said, "Longest journey for anyone in life is journey inward." Rakesh completed his inner journey long before God called upon him. I think God needed a great helper, and he got it. His life was so much full of compassion and affection that he accomplished more in twenty-three years of his life than most people in a hundred years. I am going to hold on to him, his memories, and hope that our paths will cross again.

For Rakesh, it's just the beginning, commencing toward *Moksha* and eternity. For this journey, unlike the first one, there is no turning back. One just keeps going and going until eternity.

Is he dancing his heart out in the eternity? Is he thinking of us? Is he cradled in my father and mother's arms? We all know he can sweet-talk anyone, including God.

When I am worried or distressed, is he opening his wide eyes wider and saying, "Dakshafoi, don't worry about anything. Just dance."

I know of his love for his mother and big brother. Ketki sent me these two phots from Rakesh's Instagram.

This was the Instagram Rocky had sent to his mom and big brother Amrish- around Amrish's graduation from Pharmacy school.

The women that loves me the most in this world.

Couldn't be a prouder younger brother. My elder brother exemplifies the essence of perseverance and hard work. Congrates to you Amrish Bharat Patel, Pharm D !

Chapter 18

His legacy lives on in memories and actions from family members, including children and the dance team. Even from eternity, he continuous to watch out for his parents.

In spring of 2016, Ketki and Bharat were visiting me at my Colorado home. We drove to Breckenridge for a gondola ride. Unfortunately all rides and so on were close for the public till summer. But that day was employee day, for them to ski and have a party. There was free transportation to the summit. So Ketki, Bharat, and I took the bus to the summit, where employees were having party.

After getting off from the bus, we looked around the area, took photos, and so on. Then we decided to walk to an area where employees were having a party. In front, we saw two young men walking while wearing costumes. One of them was wearing a Power Rangers costume. Immediately Ketki called him and asked if we could have a photo taken with him. After the photo, Ketki and Bharat started crying. Next to Superman, Power Rangers were his most favorite character, hence his love for bright colors, including the Power Rangers neon green costume color. As if, Rakesh was letting his parents know that he loves them.

A letter written by his cousin one year later reads,

11/6/15

Jai Swaminarayan Kaka and Kaki,

Sharing with you some of the proud moments that our kids have of their Rakeshmama.

First, let me start with Meghna. Meghna had to do a project on honoring a person that is in heaven but still makes a difference in your life. She picked her Rakeshmama and worked hard on the project. She presented her essay to the school with tears in her eyes, and her teacher was so impressed that she got 115 percent out of 100 percent. Please see the attached picture of her presentation box. Inside the box was whatever she had of her Rakeshmama: Pokemon cards, his T-shirt that she has of him, his school pictures, his Superman cape, and so on. Very very proud of her for doing this entire project on her own without anyone's help.

And secondly, Neal has a Wall of Fighters at his HST wing (Health Science Technology), and he did a leukemia project and dedicated it to his Rakeshmama. His teacher was so impressed by Neal that he did a ribbon ceremony honoring Rakesh and said it was so impactful that this entire wall would be written with his fight against cancer, and while everyone gets red ribbons, Neal got to pick a ribbon color of his choice. Of course we all know what color Neal would have picked, as you see in the pictures attached.

And on a funny note, I had taken Neelam to her physical examination appt yesterday, and Dr. Ahmed asked her if she has a boyfriend, and she answered with confidence, "No. I do not, as I promised my Rakeshmama that I would not have a boyfriend and will focus on my studies first." Dr. Ahmed was shocked to hear a teenager telling her this. She told her how proud her mama must be of her.

This is the impact Rakesh has left our kids with. I am sure their Mama is looking down from Akshardham and must be so proud of them all. Children loved him, and he loved children. I asked them to write a letter to their uncle.

Dear Rakesh Mama,

Hey it's yo fav niece, D-Dawg. Just kidding. It's Diya. I just want to say thanks for everything you have done for me, such as taking us ice skating and "paying" for the massage we gave u. I remember during the Robbinsville Mandir Mahotsav that we thought that we made up a "fake" phone number, but it was actually a real number. Ever since you passed away, I have tried to stay strong, but couldn't. Because of this, I started listening to Penn Masala. I feel like I have become more sad and upset without you around to FaceTime. You always made me laugh and make my day happier. Now for the memories and fun that we had together:

Memory #1. I remember the time when we were in Robbinsville and we left early because all of us were really tired. The traffic was really bad, and we sat in the car for about three hours before getting out of the parking lot. While we tried to get out, you fell asleep about three to four times for twenty to twenty-five minutes at a time. Rayna Didi and I laughed so much at you and your open mouth until Amrish Mama told us to let you sleep. That's one good one.

Memory #2. The next one was when we stayed at that house in Robbinsville. I was being really loud and stomping around for some reason. You told Rayna Didi and me that there was a witch downstairs and that she would turn me into a frog if I stomped around and talked loud. That's when I stopped. The next day, Rayna Didi and I went downstairs to say sorry. We expected to see a legit witch, but instead of seeing a witch's hat and ugly moles on her face, we saw a ba that looked like an average ba. I said sorry to her, and then she gave lollipops. She even asked Rayna Didi if she wanted chai. I guess your plan to shut me up backfired, but kudos to you for trying :)

Memory #3. The next one I have of us was that day when we drove the entire state of Texas (well, it kinda felt like we did) and we went to In-N-Out. I also remember asking you for a hat and some stickers 'cause I was obsessed with stickers (which I still am).

I just wanted to remember all the good memories with you. Also just saying I cried a little inside but laughed on the outside with the funny moments :\ I love and miss you tons. I wish you the best in Akshardham. I hope you are having fun playing basketball with all the gurus.

From yo fav niece,

D-DAWG (out)

05/29/17

Dear Rakesh Mama,

There's a lot that I want to say to you, just not a lot of time to write. So I'll just keep it short and sweet. I just wanted to tell you that I am eating a lot of bagels with cream cheese lathered all over it, which is healthier than a veggie sandwich with loads and loads of cheese, I think. Just kidding (inside joke).

Anyways, I really miss you. Even though I don't cry, I do miss you. I don't really know how to show you that I miss you though. Sometimes I call your phone just so I feel like you're still with us, and I pretend that you can't answer your phone because your life is getting busy with school and life in general. I guess that everyone has their own way of coping with loss.

As I write this letter, I am trying to remember all of those great memories we had together. There're just so many I have of us having so much fun! Like that time it felt like we drove around the entire state of Texas. We went from your house, to that ice sculpture place, to the In-N-Out (where Diya got her little hat and stickers), to Daksha Ba's house to hang for a bit, and then back home. I remember that day so vividly because I had so much fun with you. The ice thing was so much fun! I remember having to put on those huge ponchos and walking around, being bored. Then we got to the snow-tubing slopes. I remember thinking that it was so amazing that they put now indoors :)

However, that wasn't the best part of the experience. The best was when the four of us—Mom, Diya, me, and you—got in one tube and went down (which happened over again for about four times). After we got tired, we went to the Dunkin Donuts, which was *inside* the tubing/sculptures place and got hot chocolate. I was pretty bummed to leave because I knew that our fun day was over :(

Now the part that I don't really like to talk about, the last time I saw you. It was the day that we were leaving Dallas after Amrish Mama and Krish Mami's wedding. We were sitting in the kitchen and just talking. You seemed really annoyed about something. I remember thinking, *Why is he acting like this? What's his problem?* Before you get all offended, you have to remember how old I was. I didn't understand what you were going through, but now I do, and I feel really bad about what I was thinking.

That's not the worst thing that I regret from that day though. The thing that I most regret is not giving you a hug before we left. I know that earlier in the letter I said that I don't cry, but when I think of this, I do cry. As I wrote that line, I cried because, now seeing it written down, I realize that I took you for granted. I didn't realize that you passing away could be a reality at the time, and now that it's become one, I can't believe myself for being so stupid. I didn't think, as usual, and that cost me the last time that I could hug you. I'm so sorry for all of my actions that may have made you feel bad at any time. I really do regret it. I would give anything to see you again and apologize in person. Although I never said it to you, I do love you with all my heart. It would be a little weird if I did say it, like straight up, but it's true. I love you as if you were my older brother (even though you're my Mama). Thank you for having so much fun with me and taking care of me.

Love you so much and miss you,

Rayna

This time, the letter is from Neelam.

My object speech is about a pillow, but not just any pillow. A pillow that means the world to me. It all started when my youngest uncle was diagnosed with acute lymphoblastic leukemia cancer. It was a shock for my family. But he stayed strong and always smiled through this life-altering transition. I was frightened, but his smile secured me.

One year passed with successful remission, but suddenly his cancer got worse along with pain. Ever since he got diagnosed at the age of nineteen, we called him our Superman. Not only was he my hero, he was our whole family's superhero. A superhero rescues people in distress. But our superhero held us together in the most difficult times. Normally a person would play victim, but he rose above all and showed us what strength is. We use pillows to put our tired heads down at the end of the day. So while he was going through his rough patch, all I thought was to make him something that he could rest his tired head on, and what more to rest than what I saw him as my superhero, my Superman.

So over winter break, I made him a fleece pillow filled with love and Poly-Fil. So while he was in isolation at the hospital, we could still have a way to connect. Although he only had my pillow for a week before he passed away, the Superman pillow lays safely and peacefully in my room.

Jsn.

I am Meghana, Rakesh's nieece. We all know that Rakeshmama would always be laughing and goofing around, and most of all, he was always smiling.

My Mama always brings smiles to other faces and would brighten up their day. I remember when we were all little. Mama used to pick us up, let go, and then catch us. I would be so scared, but used to look forward to them. I also remember the time all of us would watch Rakeshmama do finger tricks. He would pretend that he pulled his fingers off.

Recently Neelam and I were taking about that and how, when we met with him, we would do that trick so Mama would smile. I know that Mama was suffering, but now I know he is in a better place. I know that Rakeshmama will always be there for us.

Love you, Rakeshmama!

Recently Shreya, who was very close to Rakesh, wrote to me that she was on her way to anesthesia residency. She added Rakesh was the first one to call her "doctor," well before she was in medical school. That's how much faith he had in her ability.

Shreya also informed me that her brother, Amit, who followed in her footsteps and enrolled at the University of Houston, had posted the following Facebook status as a captain of Roarin' Rass. She also informed me that he and the team had become nationally competitive.

Roarin' Rass: Facebook posting

"On this day almost at this time 3 years ago, the world lost one of the most impactful people that has ever existed. Rakesh- Rocky Patel. You continue and will always be one of our strongest influences in the decisions we make every day. Not one moment passes in which we don't think about you. Everything Roarin' Rass has worked tremendously hard these past 6 years for, has always been for you as we strive to continue your legacy every year, month and day. Without your actions, we wouldn't have known where to start. We probably would have never met. We may even have had different name! We miss you so much Rocky and desire to spread your enthusiastic smile and your awareness of #just dance. You are the one who taught us the most important lesson of how to bring passion onto stage and throughout our lives. The world may have lost one of the most important people ever, but your spirit resides in all of us and we wish to make you proud of Roarin' Rass continues to exist. Thank you is not enough to be greatful for everything you have done for this team Rocky. We wish you the best and love you tremendously Rocky!"

The Rass culture he established is going strong, even though original team members have graduated and moved on.

They used competition called "Space city Rass" to raise awareness and have people sign up for bone marrow donation. According to Ketki, at least forty to fifty people signed up for bone marrow donation. Imagine how proud Rakesh is while looking down from heaven of the dance team he established. His legacy is still going strong. Yes, Rakesh is alive and well, inspiring people to be generous and to help others who are in need.

This event was published in *Indo American News* on February 8, 2018.

Space City Raas Partners with Kalakriti Performing Arts for the First Garba/Raas Competition

By Nakita Pandya

HOUSTON: The University of Houston's Space City Raas (SCR) in partnership with Kalakriti Performing Arts put on an outstanding show this last weekend at Cullen Performance Hall! Eight Raas Garba teams from Texas, Missouri, Florida, and Pennsylvania traveled far and wide to compete and earn bid points to Raas All-Stars, the Raas National Championship. An exciting RAS video played at the show, presenting their event as its tenth anniversary, coming this March in Dallas.

The Space City Raas board is a group of Roarin' Raas alumni, dedicated to continuing the legacy of their founder, brother, and standing example on what it means to be a teammate, Rakesh 'Rocky' Patel. To commemorate him, the board invited the Be the Match Foundation to the show. Be the Match is operated by the National Marrow Donor Program, and has managed the largest and most diverse marrow registry in the world for the past 25 years. Space City Raas highlighted that matches found for South Asian patients are less than 3%. Their heartwarming and informative speech before intermission led to many audience viewers to register for bone marrow donation.

The dance performances were beyond energetic and enigmatic. Each team was composed of a mix of Raas and Garba songs, and included an incorporation of thematic elements. For example, Texas A&M Wreckin' Raas incorporated themes of an airport throughout their entire performance, ending their dance with a clever line alluding to their lost luggage. SLU Raas, from Saint Louis University, traveled through a Supermarket in their dance, showing them going down the aisles and grabbing common grocery. All of these themes accompanied a combination of traditional Gujarati folk dance and modern influences. These performances were a perfect of example of the Indian-American youth, and their drive to preserve their two cultures.

An array of Judges were picked for Choreography, Execution, and Artistic Element. The talented Kusum Sharma from Kalakriti Performing Arts was one of two Artistic Element judges, using her experience and knowledge on Indian dance to decide her top choices. All of the judges went through thorough judges training, as well as an exciting judges deliberation after all the performances were done. They went through each and every opinion until the there was a consensus.

While the judges spent time deliberating their top choices, to beautifully arranged dance pieces went into motion. One was a classical dance team from Sunanda Nair Performing Arts, and the other was a Bollywood dance organized by Kusum Sharma's Shri Natraj School of Dance. Both performances showcased differing Indian styles of dance! At the end of it only one team came out on top, and that team was University of Texas, Dallas, TaRaas. In second and third place were UT Texas Raas and UF GatoRaas, respectively. Families and friends from all over Texas came to watch an unforgettable show. From high-energy performances, to meaningful and charitable speeches, Space City Raas was an event that created a lasting impression on a diverse audience.

Kalakriti Performing Arts is non-profit organization with mission to support Indian culture and heritage through artistic and visual dance forms. Over the years Kalakriti has worked with several other Houston non-profit organizations to support their fundraiser.